'I love this book. It is easy to read, the pec
down the gospel in a way that not only brir
faith and a desire to be a relentless advoca'
new Christian alike. Bravo to the Evangel
Revd Celia Apeagyei-Collins, founder an

CW01507828

'In a world where identity crises abour
and Knox use a creative and rich mix of story, testimony, history, encourage....
further, and an underpinning of theology to enable evangelicals and others to understand
their identity in a world that can be hostile and a Church that can be confused. This book is
challenging, joyful, sad, stimulating, motivating, humbling and always Christ centred. While
some seek to redefine evangelicalism, the authors helpfully revisit core definitions of what it
means to be an evangelical.'
Revd Chris Briggs, Chair, Methodist Evangelicals Together (MET: Revive)

'What a book! Excitingly biblical, remarkably contemporary and profoundly relevant to our
church, country, culture and local community. This book really is authentic good news about
Good News people ... the Church of Jesus Christ. The book is saturated with hope!

With refreshing honesty and prophetic insight, Gavin and Phil have given us a gold mine.
From their vast personal experience and drone-like perspective of God's people across the
United Kingdom, they have given us a superb resource. In a society where we are so often
tiptoeing in minefields, this book is full of visionary signposts, probing challenges and
immense encouragement.'
Bishop Ken Clarke, former Bishop of Kilmore, Elphin and Ardagh

'Gavin Calver and Phil Knox provide an amazing clarification of what the gospel means and
how to understand the context to share it in unity and increasing collaboration. I thoroughly
recommend this new contribution, which demonstrates both a deep understanding of the
reality of the evangelical church in the UK and the practical experience of two passionate
evangelists, who have shared the gospel in different contexts of spiritual, social and cultural
backgrounds.'
Dr Samuel Cueva, missiologist, church leader and writer

'I could not put this book down. I absolutely loved it and will be recommending it to everyone.
Thank you Gavin and Phil for such a comprehensive and compassionate framework for the
essential characteristics of evangelical Christianity, combined with five clear and compelling
applications for everyday disciples of Jesus Christ. Terrific!'
Dr Graham Daniels, General Director, Christians in Sport and Director, Cambridge United FC

'Living in a world that's looking for truth, this book is very insightful, clear and brings clarity
to the purpose of Christians who are passionate about sharing Jesus and his gospel.'
Revd Canon Les Isaac OBE, founder and President of the Ascension Trust

'*Good News People* is a rallying cry for every believer who wonders where they fit in today's
world. With their signature warmth and clarity, Gavin Calver and Phil Knox remind us that

being evangelical is not just a theological label – it's a calling to be carriers of hope in a culture gripped by uncertainty. This book is both an encouragement and a challenge. It calls us to stand firm in our faith, yet move with grace and boldness into a world longing for real hope. It reminds us that we are part of a bigger story – one written by the hand of God and carried forward by those willing to be brave, kind, united and unashamed of the good news we bear. If you need fresh confidence in the gospel and your place in God's mission, this is the book to read.'
Pastor Preethy Kurian, Senior Pastor, Capstone Church, Ilford

'*Good News People* is a compelling call to an evangelical unity that holds firm to the authority of Scripture, the centrality of the cross, and the lordship of Christ, while also remaining engaged with the world around us. Gavin Calver and Phil Knox challenge us to embody the good news of the gospel we share, reflecting the love of Jesus, holding firm to the counter-cultural truths of his Lordship, and sharing the hope found in him alone. This is an important book for any who long to see the gospel proclaimed with clarity, conviction and compassion by churches, organisations and individual Christians united in Christ.'
Matt Lillicrap, CEO, UCCF

'*Good News People* is an inspiring and practical read for anyone passionate about sharing the gospel. Written by two top men of God in our nation today, this book equips readers with faith-filled wisdom and biblical grounding to engage today's culture with truth and grace. It encourages and challenges us to play our part in building God's church, spreading the good news with confidence, kindness and conviction. A must-read!'
Jay Lusted, Lead Pastor, Festival Church Old Colwyn, actor and TV presenter

'*Good News People* is a timely and urgent call to embrace the hope, unity and boldness of the gospel in our generation. With contagious passion and keen insight, Gavin and Phil weave together compelling stories, rich theological depth and practical wisdom to inspire believers to stand firm and shine brightly. This book is both an encouragement and a challenge – a powerful reminder that evangelicalism, at its core, is about standing on the truth of Scripture, proclaiming the life-changing message of Jesus, and living out our faith with courage and compassion.

Whether you are a church leader, a new believer, or someone longing to see God move in fresh ways, *Good News People* will stir your heart, strengthen your faith and equip you to carry the good news into a world that desperately needs it. I highly recommend it!'
Revd Nims Obunge MBE DL, Senior Pastor, Freedoms Ark, Tottenham and CEO of The Peace Alliance

'*Good News People* explores what it means to be an evangelical Christian in contemporary society, especially within the UK context. Speaking about how we can navigate a "permacrisis", it points out that we have a message of hope in an increasingly volatile era. As a ship needs a compass or the stars to find true north, this book emphasises how evangelical identity can remain fundamentally faithful to the gospel – the good news – and remain relevant without "selling out". The authors advocate unity amidst diversity, pushing believers to "stand stronger and reach higher". I would highly recommend it.'
Revd Yinka Oyekan, Team Leader, Evangelical Baptists and Senior Minister, The Gate, Reading

'*Good News People* arrives as a timely manifesto for the Church as we navigate cultural complexities with both courage and grace. This compelling book challenges us to be brave yet kind, culturally relevant without compromise and realistically hopeful in our witness. This wonderful book both inspires and equips us to make Jesus known with renewed clarity and conviction in today's rapidly changing landscape.'
Revd Mark Pugh, General Superintendent, Elim Pentecostal Church and Apostolic Lead, Rediscover Church, Exeter

'It is difficult to think of a more important book to read at this juncture. It touches on a host of super relevant themes. Gavin and Phil articulate evangelical values for a new generation this side of the Atlantic. A must read for those who want to be relevant in the public square for this generation.'
Bishop Mike Royal, General Secretary, Churches Together in England

'Some Christian leaders exhibit a remarkable awareness of a given cultural moment. Others share great enthusiasm for encouraging signs among churches, but often without this awareness. In this book you get both. With deep insight and gospel vision, Gavin Calver and Phil Knox pool their extensive experience to proclaim that "God is on the move in the UK church". Yes, we see many challenges in the Western church today. But we also know that our God is on the move advancing his mission in our time. This book gives the good news story of that advance.'
Dr Ed Stetzer, Dean, Talbot School of Theology at Biola University and Scholar in Residence and Teaching Pastor, Mariners Church, Anaheim

'It is all too easy for evangelicals in Britain to feel discouraged. The mainstream churches are in rapid decline, creating a post-Christian and secular culture. Evangelicals are small in number and influence, often viewed as bigoted for their views on human sexuality and mistakenly assumed to share the outlook of the US Republican Party. The national roles that Gavin and Phil have with Evangelical Alliance enable them to tell a better story, and it is an encouraging one. Drawing on their first-hand experiences, they report that evangelicals are growing and diverse. They make a vital contribution to the life of the community, tackling issues of poverty and injustice. While evangelical churches undoubtedly face significant challenges, they also have great opportunities, which Gavin and Phil urge them to grasp. They define evangelicalism biblically, and call evangelicals to stand firm for their doctrinal convictions. They emphasise the need to be brave and kind, and to show the contemporary relevance of the faith. Their warm appreciation of the history of the Evangelical Alliance means they highlight the vital importance of fostering evangelical unity. This is a book that every evangelical ought to read. It will warm our hearts, cause our faith to rise, and provides a manifesto for action to meet the needs of our times. May the Lord help us to be the hopeful gospel people Gavin and Phil envisage. This is what our nation needs above all else.'
John Stevens, National Director, Fellowship of Independent Evangelical Churches (FIEC)

'When every "Insta reel" is a new influencer, with a new brand, face cream or fitness plan, Gavin and Phil unpack what it means to be evangelical influencers for Jesus, rather than the influenced. I love that they encourage us that "It's so simple, and possible, to be culturally relevant without selling out on our content."

'*Good News People* is a book of hope! Gavin and Phil so clearly write revealing their burning hearts for the church to work collaboratively to share the good news and together make Jesus known. They explain succinctly what it means to be evangelical, as well as giving us a brief and fascinating short history of the evangelical alliance. Their stories are a shot in the arm of hope and encouragement about the state of the evangelical church across the UK. I feel more inspired to share my faith, be courageous in what I believe in, and to live boldly and kindly.'
Dr Chloe Swart, National Director of Alpha UK

'Gavin and Phil's book feels like being guided to sure footing in rocky terrain. It has filled me with fresh joy, courage and hope: instead of fear about how I'll be perceived as an evangelical, *Good News People* has reminded me of the joy of bearing that name. Instead of feeling pushed back, it's poured courage into me to press on; instead of despair at the state of our broken world, it's energised me with renewed hope that there is a hunger for the gospel. Above all, Good News People has inspired me afresh to keep my eyes firmly fixed on Jesus and to take every opportunity to tell others about how wonderful he is.'
Natalie Williams, CEO, Jubilee+

'Reading this book is like breathing pure oxygen. As you turn the pages, strength, hope, encouragement and courage fill your heart and spirit. This book encourages us to hold firm to the power of the gospel, the power of the Bible and the power of Christian activism at a time of crisis, loneliness and uncertainty. Mostly it's a book of hope. God is on the move. The times are serious, but the times are changing and the time for a Jesus movement is now.'
Ness Wilson, Pioneer UK Leader and Team Leader, Open Heaven Church, Loughborough

'This book is a must read, filled with faith-building stories. In these difficult times Gavin and Phil bring real hope and compelling vision. They celebrate the move of God taking place in unexpected places across the Evangelical Church in the UK, highlighting the Good News amidst all the noise. They urge us to stand firm on God's word and our calling to share the Gospel. As we navigate the way ahead, the postures they encourage evangelicals to adopt are really empowering. In reading this book, I've been struck by how exciting it is to realise the collective power of this vibrant and growing community.'
Debby Wright, National Director of Vineyard Churches UK and Ireland and founding pastor, Trent Vineyard, Nottingham

'These days the term "evangelical" leads to all sorts of responses and associations – not all positive. In *Good News People*, Calver and Knox help us recalibrate to the term's true meaning – centred around the good news of the crucified, risen and reigning Lord Jesus. As a church pastor, I found the book relevant and encouraging, relating to both the joys and challenges of seeking to make Jesus known in the world today. It brings a positive message of hope.'
Revd Jago Wynne, Rector, Holy Trinity Clapham

GOOD NEWS PEOPLE

HOPEFUL EVANGELICALS YESTERDAY, TODAY and TOMORROW

GAVIN CALVER and PHIL KNOX

INTER-VARSITY PRESS
SPCK Group, Studio 101, The Record Hall, 16–16A Baldwin's Gardens, London EC1N
7RJ, England
Email: ivp@ivpbooks.com
Website: www.ivpbooks.com

First published 2025

EU GPSR Authorised Representative
LOGOS EUROPE, 9 rue Nicolas Poussin, 17000, LA ROCHELLE, France
E-mail: Contact@logoseurope.eu

British Library Cataloguing-in-Publication Data
A catalogue record for this book is available from the British Library.

ISBN hbk: 978–1–78974–565–8
ISBN pbk: 978–1–78974–566–5
eBook ISBN: 978–1–78974–567–2

Set in Minion Pro 10.35/13.75 pt
Typeset in Great Britain by Fakenham Prepress Solutions, Fakenham, Norfolk NR21 8NL
Printed in Great Britain by Clays Ltd, Bungay, Suffolk

Produced on paper from sustainable forests

*Inter-Varsity Press publishes Christian books that are true to the Bible and that
communicate the gospel, develop discipleship and strengthen the church for its mission in
the world.*

*IVP originated within the Inter-Varsity Fellowship, now the Universities and Colleges
Christian Fellowship, a student movement connecting Christian Unions in universities
and colleges throughout Great Britain, and a member movement of the International
Fellowship of Evangelical Students. Website: www.uccf.org.uk. That historic association is
maintained, and all senior IVP staff and committee members subscribe to the UCCF Basis
of Faith.*

Dedication

To the broad shoulders of the good news people who have gone before us, on whose legacy we stand.

Acknowledgements

We have loved writing this book together. It's a joy to serve at the Evangelical Alliance and we've really enjoyed digging into some of the history of this ministry as well as putting down on paper what it means to be the kind of hopeful evangelicals needed in our day. We are grateful for many friends who've helped us along the way, especially those who've allowed us to share their stories or kindly read earlier versions of the manuscript and helped shape the book profoundly with their feedback. We are so thankful to our wonderful wives, Anne and Dani, for all their support and challenge throughout writing this book.

We are very grateful to all the team at IVP and to Tom Creedy in particular for such incredible help along the way. We thank our friends, families and churches for their sharing of the journey and for all the encouragement given as we wrote this.

As co-authors, we have contributed to every chapter. When the story in the chapter ends, the writer may well change, but be assured that every sentence has been agreed together. We are both most certainly hopeful evangelicals. We pray that this book will help you to be one of these too.

Enjoy the read!

Contents

Foreword

I love it when an old word comes back to life.

Five hundred years ago, when Martin Luther retranslated 'do penance', it was a gateway discovery which excavated Jesus's invitation from under centuries of religiosity: 'Repent, it's good news, the Kingdom of God is near' (Mark 1:15).

Gavin Calver and Phil Knox have a unique vantage point for discovering buried treasure as they visit church families across England, Scotland, Wales and Northern Ireland in their work for the Evangelical Alliance (EA).

This book is the fruit of these travels. And in it they bring an old word back to life.

The name 'Evangelical' has lots of resonances. Occasionally, there can be a shadow side where we become defined religiously by what we're against rather than what we're enthusiastically for.

But I love their retranslation: Good News People.

In my early years of Christian leadership, in my beloved denomination not known for its passion, I found myself repeatedly apologising for my enthusiasm. My spiritual mother put her finger on this: 'Jill, never apologise for your enthusiasm: the word comes from the Greek *en-theos* meaning full of God'. Not long afterwards, I recall an early speaking engagement for New Wine at St George's, Leeds. I had to rush away at the end to get back home for my boys, but a couple made a beeline for me, catching me as I escaped through the door and saying, 'We'll be quick. We just have to tell you this. Never apologise for your enthusiasm.'

So I make no apology for my enthusiasm for *Good News People*. I make no apology for my enthusiasm for my thirty years as a member of the Evangelical Alliance. The EA is good news for good news people, who believe in the authority of the Bible, the significance of the cross, the need to make decisions and the desire to make a difference

As a member of the EA council, I treasure our annual 24-hour retreat with a much-loved, colour-filled range of senior Christian leaders from across the British Isles. In the crosswinds of culture, the EA's role is as vital as ever: to unite the Church to reach the lost in every corner of the United Kingdom and give the Church a clear, united, confident and effective voice in every layer of society.

So fasten your seat belts, and travel the UK with Gavin and Phil, who are enthusiastic and authentic navigators of the valleys as well as the mountaintops.

Here are my highlights from their tour de force. There's something for everyone. (You might even catch their enthusiasm for five-a-side football!)

The tide is turning. The seasons are changing. The permafrost of secularism is melting. The openness to the gospel is profound. The *Talking Jesus* report (2022) showed that 1 in 3 non-Christians were open to a conversation about the Christian faith, after meeting a Christian friend. In their latest study, *Finding Jesus* (2025) the EA were looking for 100 adults to share their recent experience of coming to faith. They were inundated with three times that number of stories. When participants were asked 'Which aspect of the gospel most drew you to Jesus?', the most compelling attraction was that 'Jesus loves me.'

And, wonderfully, we find this deeply buried in the founding story of the Evangelical Alliance. On 1 October 1845, 216 Christian leaders met together in Liverpool's Medical Hall. Congregationalist John Angell James spoke prophetically, 'Every chorus of human voices depends on the "keynote" being rightly struck, and the keynote that must be struck now is love.'

Both Gavin and Phil weave in personal stories of being Good News People who are brave and kind. I would have loved to be one of Phil's neighbours with his Easter egg extravanganza; I was inspired by Gavin's hinge moment where he was specifically called to be brave, and step out of his work for *Youth for Christ*.

Gavin and Phil speak compellingly of hope with realism. Gavin speaks of the Church in the UK which 'used to be more of a set menu but is now becoming a buffet.' They see an astonishing flourishing of church planting and entrepreneurial mission happening. While, for some, it's a hard season with pressure and challenges. When Gavin took time to personally phone each of the thirty churches who hadn't renewed their subscription to the EA, for twenty eight of them, it was because they had closed or were closing. But for every church that is closing, people are starting new churches to reach God's lost sons and daughters.

A key opportunity for innovation is the digital world, where the information superhighway lays tracks for the gospel just as in the earliest days of Christianity, the gospel spread via the Roman roads. For example, one pastor told them: 'I've had more unchurched people come to church in the last six months through TikTok than through personal invitation.' The online service is the row behind the back row.

The *Finding Jesus* research shows that the second most popular way to come to faith is still by people reading the Bible. But in first place is 'an experience of God'. As they travel the UK, Gavin and Phil notice a significant upsurge in people becoming Christians without any human intervention, inspired to explore faith by dreams or being drawn by a supernatural force. As they say, 'Jesus is reminding us that he is the best evangelist.' At one church, they report, a university student turned up on the church steps explaining he had woken with an overwhelming burden to 'repent'. At another, an older woman told the story of how she had sensed God prompting her to walk into the doors of the church in her village each time she passed it – she dared to go in and her heart was warmed by the welcome. Historian and author Tom Holland observes from outside the Church in an episode of Justin Brierley's podcast *The Surprising Rebirth of Belief in God*:

> The area of growth seems to be churches that take the supernatural seriously … that take angels and signs from God and miracles seriously. I don't understand why anyone would be interested in a Christianity that isn't taking this stuff seriously.[1]

Every time I see Gavin and Phil, or phone for some help or advice, they are unfailingly compassionate, supportive and enthusiastic. In the corridors of power of Westminster, Holyrood, the Senedd or Stormont, they are courageous and gracious as they contend for the renewal of our nations. As you meet them on the pages of this good news book, I am confident they'll make you feel part of the family, reassured when the journey is exhausting, and encouraged by the buried treasure they have found on their travels. I am so thankful to God for these Good News People – full of Jesus.

Rt Revd Dr Jill Duff
Anglican Bishop of Lancaster, Chair of New Wine England

---

1 J. Brierley and T. Holland 'Are We Witnessing a Rebirth of belief in God?', *The Surprising Rebirth of Belief in God*, season 1, episode 9, https://www.youtube.com/watch?v=VG6xIvxrd20 (accessed 17 April 2025).

Introduction

Everyone has inside of them a piece of good news. The good news is that you don't know how great you can be! How much you can love! What you can accomplish! And what your potential is!
Anne Frank[1]

'How did it go today mate?'

Almost every Sunday one of us sends a text message like this to the other. One of the best bits of our jobs is preaching in a different church most weeks, encouraging communities of faith and spending time listening to leaders. We go where we are invited, but on any given Sunday, we can be anywhere in the UK, ministering in contexts as broad and diverse as the population. And to our delight, what we have come to expect is that almost every reply to this text over the last few years has been effervescent with encouragement (and this is not just because of the enthusiasm of their authors!).

After a while we realised that we had a story to tell about what God is doing and the people who are part of it.

God is on the move in the UK Church. This book is a good news story.

Hardly anyone else gets to see what we are privileged to see. Our work at the Evangelical Alliance gives us a unique bird's eye view of the landscape of the Church across England, Scotland, Wales and Northern Ireland. But we also see the perils as well as the potential,

---

1 L. Tscherry, 'Anne Frank: 10 Beautiful Quotes from The Diary of a Young Girl', *The Guardian*, 27 January 2015, https://www.theguardian.com/childrens-books-site/2015/jan/27/the-greatest-anne-frank-quotes-ever (accessed 19 December 2024).

the pitfalls as well as the possibilities. We have walked with leaders through the heartaches as well as the highs.

We live in a contested space. There is a posture we need to hold in this cultural moment.

When it comes to life and faith, we need somewhere solid on which to stand and something ambitious to strive for. We need a firm foundation on which we can fix our feet and a compelling vision on which we can set our gaze. We need the safety of a true story in which we find our place and the adventure of being part of the writing of the chapters to come.

We believe that these two elements are found not only in knowing Jesus as Lord and Saviour, but specifically in being an evangelical. Our aim in this book is to inspire you to stand stronger and reach higher, to be braver and kinder, to have a firmer footing and a more hopeful outlook.

We believe that this is true for you personally, but we also believe it applies to the world in which we live. As we look at our newsfeeds, the headlines are as bad as at any other moment in our lifetimes. The *Collins Dictionary* word of the year for 2022 was 'permacrisis'.[2] This is defined as 'an extended period of instability and insecurity', especially one resulting from a series of catastrophic events. For many people, there is an anxiety-inducing sense that we have lurched from a global pandemic to a cost-of-living crisis, the threat of another world war, ecological meltdown, political instability and a loneliness epidemic. As the times become increasingly volatile, so do our needs, and also our society's desire for deep rootedness in a truth and a hopeful assurance that everything will be all right in the end.

This book is about firm foundations and audacious hope. To be good news people is to hold these two facets of faith together. This

---

2 D. Shariatmadari, 'A Year of Permacrisis', *Collins Dictionary*, 1 November 2022, https://blog.collinsdictionary.com/language-lovers/a-year-of-permacrisis/ (accessed 19 December 2024).

is the journey we want to take you on. We are going to 'look' in five different directions:

- In Part 1, we will encourage you to look *down* at the ground on which we stand, exploring the core of evangelicalism and what we believe defines us as good news people. But we will affirm that we do not do so alone. This is also a book about unity. We will ask you to look *around* at the Jesus-followers around you, across denominations, backgrounds, ages and ethnicities, as well as looking *back* at our story. We will see that our brushstroke is but one in a masterpiece of the Creator. (We will use the terms 'evangelicals' and 'good news people' interchangeably throughout the book.)
- In Part 2, we will ask you to lift your eyes to see what the Lord is doing in the UK at this present time. While Part 1 invites us to look down at the terrain on which we stand, Part 2 beckons us to look *up* at the wider landscape and look *forward* to the future of the Church. Alongside the permacrisis, we perceive a remarkable work of God in the Church and every week we meet people whose lives have been transformed by Jesus. This book will tell you a different story to the one you hear in the secular media about the state and health of the Church in this nation.

At the heart of this section are five 'postures' that we believe we must hold to be faithful and fruitful in this season. We will invite you to reflect on how you are standing, as we identify the disciplines and habits necessary for hopeful evangelicals in this season. We will also consider how we can cultivate cultures and communities of good news people, knowing that whatever our level of influence, we all have a part to play in this area. As we draw the threads of the book together, we hope you will turn the last page with steel in your bones and fire in your heart.

The overarching story you will hear is one we are bursting to tell. We both have unusual callings. We are both rooted in local churches but are often absent on a Sunday morning. In the last few years, we have both spoken in churches from almost every denomination in almost every UK context: urban and rural, old and young, sometimes to hundreds, sometimes to handfuls. Occasionally, we are the only white people in the room; occasionally, there are *only* white people in the room. In some places, we are perceived as young; elsewhere, we are seen as old. Sometimes we have to rein in our enthusiasm and give time to a patient translator as we speak to congregations for whom English is not their first language. More than most, we get to foretaste heaven as we see the beautifully rich diversity across the evangelical world on a weekly basis. All of these ongoing experiences have given us a unique and valuable vantage point from which to observe and report. We hope you will enjoy standing with us as we share exciting snapshots from the Church in this nation.

We also hope to embody the unity and passion for the gospel we long for in how we communicate in this book. We are writing as likeminded and wholehearted evangelists, whose burning hearts long for the Church to work collaboratively to share the good news and together make Jesus known. But your authors are also great friends and have ministered together for almost twenty years. Great things are not achieved in isolation. Life is a team game, not an individual pursuit. We hope that as you read this book, it will feel like you are listening in on a dialogue between its authors, and on countless conversations with leaders over many years and miles of ministry.

We believe that the message of this book – to stand strong in our evangelical call and identity – is both timeless and timely. It is timeless in the sense that, as we will see, we as 'good news people' stand on the shoulders of 'good news giants' – those who have partnered with God throughout history to strengthen his people and bring gospel joy to countless others. But it is also a timely moment, as we reel from a permacrisis, as our neighbours and colleagues search for meaning and as we face unprecedented challenges on individual, societal and global levels. Into this vacuum of hope, we live and tell the glorious story of the One who loves us and gave himself for us. He gives us the firmest of foundations on which to build our lives and unrivalled assurance for our future. The world has never needed it more.

So, our invitation to you is to join us on this journey. Will you celebrate with us the joy of being a good news person in a bad news world? Will you allow us to enthuse you and encourage you with stories of transformation from across the UK Church? And will you grapple with the tensions we present and listen to the Spirit challenging and nudging you to grow in faithfulness and fruitfulness in this cultural moment?

You will notice that this book is called *Good News People*, not *Good News Person*. Like most things in life, it is best read in community. With this in mind, we have designed some small group resources with discussion questions and fun activities to enhance and apply the learning from the book. You can find these along with supplementary videos and more at www.goodnewspeople. church.

Part I
WHAT WE BELIEVE

1

Evangelicals – who are we?

> Evangelicalism is, above all, historic Christian orthodoxy combined with energetic fervour to promote the gospel of Jesus Christ.
>
> Michael Bird[1]

I, Gavin, live in London, which means that I do not need a car most of the week. However, at the weekend I can be ministering anywhere across the country and so I frequently need a hire car. Sometimes the local Europcar likes to honour my loyalty by providing the best car they have, even though I ordered the cheapest one available. When they deliver a brand-new Mercedes, this can make arriving at an Evangelical Alliance member church interesting as I worry about the perception it might create. In some of our churches, it would be seen as honouring for me to drive such a car; in others, it would give entirely the wrong impression for the leader of the Evangelical Alliance to be driving a car that would be seen as overly flashy.

A while ago, I was due to speak in Birmingham and so set off early up the M40. Making good time, I stopped at the Warwick services for a coffee. Coffee mission accomplished, I attempted to reverse out of the car parking space to continue my journey when a large white police van with blue flashing lights pulled up behind me and blocked my exit. Two officers got out of the van, knocked on the window and asked me to get out of the car where they could see my hands.

I got out of the car and the interrogation began.

---

1 M. Bird, *Evangelical Theology: A biblical and systematic introduction*, 2nd edition (Grand Rapids: Zondervan, 2020), p. 28.

'Where did you get this stolen car from?' the policeman asked.

'Europcar,' I said.

'Where are you going?'

'To preach at a church in Birmingham.'

Calmly, I produced the paperwork and the situation was soon defused – partly because I had managed to explain myself and partly because I was dressed like an unthreatening geography teacher.

'What's going on?' I asked them.

'The car was wrongly marked as stolen on the national database. Four ANPR cameras were triggered between your home in London and the Warwick services. When you came into the service station, a warning went out for any police within ten minutes to come and apprehend the car thief.'

Relieved and back on the road, I wondered what would have happened if I had not stopped for a coffee. What if I had been apprehended as I was being welcomed at the church I was heading to?!

But here is the point: when you have the wrong information you come to the wrong conclusion.

When it comes to who we are as evangelicals, many people within and outside of the Church have come to the wrong conclusion. This chapter is about who we really are as good news people and why that identity matters.

What people hear when they hear the word 'evangelical'

I, Phil, was in a pub with a new group of friends. As conversation progressed, my faith naturally dropped into discussion. One of the men around the table asked, 'Yeah, but what type of Christian are you? You're not one of those "over the top evangelical" types, are you?' My new friend was to be disappointed.

For some, especially outside the Church, the perception of evangelicals is that they have another and unnecessary level of religious fervour. The actress Carey Mulligan was asked about her faith in an interview for *The Times* in 2024. She told her story, saying, 'I don't think I would describe myself as super-super-Christian.'[2] Within our culture, private religion is tolerated, even admired – but many are wary of 'over-the-top' expressions of faith. The word 'evangelical' is often used to describe this kind of zeal.

For others, the word 'evangelical' is synonymous with 'evangelistic'. This is an understandable mistake to make as both words share the same root. We hear people ask, 'Is it an evangelical service?' What they are often asking is whether it is aimed at giving unbelievers an opportunity to respond to the gospel – in other words, is it 'evangelistic'? But, as we are about to unpack, to be 'evangelical' means more than this.

As with any attempt to categorise people, there can be a tendency to assume that all evangelical Christians think and act alike. However, one of the most incredible things about UK evangelicalism is the rich diversity within it. In reality, we think very differently on some issues but remain united on key truths. Jonathan Lamb puts it this way, 'there are many issues over which evangelicals disagree but, to be true to that name, we must be united in our stand on the foundational truths of the gospel and in our commitment to the final authority of the Bible.'[3] More on this to come.

US and them

In recent years, the unfolding story of American politics has had a profound influence on the perception of evangelicals globally. The

2 D. Birrell, '"I'm not super, super Christian, but I go to church", says Carey Mulligan', Premier Christian News, 5 February 2024, https://premierchristian.news/en/news/article/i-m-not-super-super-christian-but-i-go-to-church-says-carey-mulligan (accessed 19 December 2024).

3 J. Lamb, *Essentially One: Striving for the unity God loves* (London: IVP, 2020), p. 40.

relationship between the evangelical community in the USA and the Republican Party is so strong and influential that it is sometimes described in terms of a marriage. One of the implications of this is that political, nationalistic and theological views have all been fused together. Political policies and decisions have been elevated and supported theologically and have come to become defining markers of evangelicals because of the strength of the political relationship.

I, Gavin, wrote about this very issue for the American publication *Newsweek*:

> Politics and faith will always be connected on some level. However, the marrying of the two so closely in recent times in the USA has been hugely problematic for us all. Poor political decisions being rigorously defended by many Christian leaders, who I have great respect for, has been painful to watch. Christians need to pray for, and support leaders, but they also need to make a stand against that which is wrong. I will always be passionate about the need for evangelical Christians to be fully engaged with public life. However, in the end the church's primary loyalty must be to Jesus and not blindly given to any national figure or leader.[4]

In the UK, things are very different. British evangelicals are not wedded to any political affiliation. We know evangelicals from all the major political parties, in senior roles and at grassroots level. In our advocacy work, we get to meet with politicians across the political spectrum. A study of British evangelicals in 2017 found that 25% of them voted Labour, 21% Conservative and 5%

---

4 J. Lemon, 'Prominent Evangelical Leader Calls Out "Absolute Wedding of Politics and Faith" in US', *Newsweek*, 2 February 2021, https://www.newsweek.com/prominent-evangelical-leader-calls-out-absolute-wedding-politics-faith-us-1566209 (accessed 19 December 2024).

Liberal Democrats; 31% said they had no party affiliation at all.[5] In the recent American election in November 2024, a huge 81% of white evangelicals voted for Trump.[6] In response to the election results, Gavin wrote in *Christianity Today*,

> we will once again have to respond to accusations from those who assume that British evangelicals marry politics and faith in the same way as those who carry the label *evangelical* in the US. Politics and faith will always be connected to a degree, but the symbiotic relationship between one's faith and one's political persuasion, with *evangelical* often being perceived as a synonym for *MAGA [Make America Great Again]*, has been hugely problematic for us in the UK.[7]

On this side of the Atlantic, seven in ten Britons hold an unfavourable opinion of Donald Trump.[8] Given this, it is easy to see how the unlikely alliance between politics and faith in the USA has negatively impacted people's perceptions of UK evangelicals by association. The theologian, David Bebbington, wrote about the differences between the USA and the UK in these terms: 'British evangelicals became less entrenched in their political partisanship than Americans. Evangelicals of the left and evangelicals changing sides were not unusual. It never became axiomatic in Britain that conservatism in theology dictated conservatism in politics.'[9]

---

5 A. C. Hatcher, *Political and Religious Identities of British Evangelicals* (London: Palgrave Macmillan, 2017).

6 R. Paveley, 'White Evangelicals Help Donald Trump to Regain the White House', *Church Times*, 6 November 2024, https://www.churchtimes.co.uk/articles/2024/8-november/news/world/white-evangelicals-help-donald-trump-to-regain-the-white-house (accessed 19 December 2024).

7 CT Editors, 'What Another Trump Presidency Means to Evangelicals around the World', *Christianity Today*, 7 November 2024, https://www.christianitytoday.com/2024/11/trump-evangelicals-global-china-israel-nepal-uk/ (accessed 19 December 2024).

8 Ipsos, '7 in 10 Britons Hold an Unfavourable Opinion of Donald Trump', 7 December 2022, https://www.ipsos.com/en-uk/7-10-britons-hold-unfavourable-opinion-donald -trump (accessed 19 December 2024).

9 M. Noll, D. Bebbington and G. Marsden (eds), *Evangelicals: Who they have been, are now, and could be* (Grand Rapids: Eerdmans, 2019), p. 299.

We love our brothers and sisters in America and love being part of a global family. There will not be a British section and an American section in heaven – there will simply be brothers and sisters. We rejoice in the growth of Christianity globally and love visiting the Church in other nations, but we have a distinct definition of what it means to be an evangelical and do not necessarily see politics in the same way as our American brothers and sisters.

Who are we really? Good news people in a bad news world

We both love the etymology of words. Tragically the origins of our names are not terribly profound. Philip means 'lover of horses' and Gavin means 'white hawk'. But there is much more cause for enthusiasm when it comes to the basis of the word 'evangelical'. It comes from the Greek root, *evangel*, which means 'good news'.

An evangelical is a good news person in a bad news world.

And in this regard, Jesus is our example and inspiration. Mark records the moment Jesus begins his ministry:

After John was put in prison, Jesus went into Galilee, proclaiming the good news of God. 'The time has come,' he said. 'The kingdom of God has come near. Repent and believe the good news!'
(Mark 1:14–15)

Here, the Greek word for good news is *euangelion*, which appears seventy-six times in the New Testament. It is either translated as 'good news', as it is here, or as 'gospel.' It is a compound word, combining *eu*, which means 'joyful', and *angelos*, which is to describe a herald of news. The gospel is news that brings joy.

Stanley J. Grenz observes, 'To be evangelical means to be centred on the gospel. Consequently, evangelicals are a gospel people.'[10] This in itself is no great surprise. As the late John Stott pointed out, 'in seeking to define what it means to be evangelical, it is inevitable that we begin with the gospel. For both our theology (evangelicalism) and our activity (evangelism) derive their meaning and their importance from the good news (the evangel).'[11]

Gavin reinforced this view in an article he wrote for *The Times* newspaper about what it means to be an evangelical.[12] He talked about how the term 'evangelical' is a good news one and how evangelicals are hugely engaged in transforming the UK socially and spiritually. He highlighted how evangelicals are part of a massive global family and the fact that most of the growing churches in the UK are evangelical and here to serve widely.

The term evangelical is not redundant – although it does need redeeming a little and we want to be part of this in the days ahead. Recent research indicates that there are currently up to 660 million evangelicals worldwide.[13] We can both see this number growing in the future.

The important thing for us will be to keep the main thing central and not get distracted by the noise around us. Many people have emphasised that the two major hallmarks of evangelicals are their being both Bible people and gospel people. Moving forward, both the Bible and the gospel are utterly vital. Vital for evangelicals – or 'good news people' – and vital for our world.

---

10 S. J. Grenz, *Renewing the Center: Evangelical theology in a post-theological era* (Grand Rapids: Baker, 2006), p. 337.

11 J. Stott, *Evangelical Truth: A personal plea for unity, integrity and faithfulness* (Carlisle: Langham Partnership, 2013), p. 11.

12 G. Calver, 'Credo', *The Times*, 16 January 2021 (accessed 23 October 2024).

13 Aaron Earls, '3 in 5 Evangelicals Live in Asia or Africa', Lifeway Research, 2 March 2020, https://research.lifeway.com/2020/03/02/3-in-5-evangelicals-live-in-asia-or-africa (accessed 19 December 2024).

What is the good news?

Naturally then, the question arises, what is the good news? How do we define it? This is an important task if it is so core to our identity. We will consider it from three different angles. First, as an announcement.

1 An announcement

I, Phil, was sitting with the leadership team of a church recently and we were agonising together about how describing oneself as an evangelical was likely to be misunderstood. One leader commented that it was interesting how those outside the Church had adopted words from the Christian subculture. For example, reporters will sometimes refer to storms of 'biblical' proportions, we may be warned not to take a piece of information as 'gospel' and, aptly, the word, 'vegangelical' was used recently to describe someone who shared passionately about their animal product-free diet. I then reflected on the fact that Christians were not the first people to use the word *euangelion*.

For example, in the city of Priene in Western Turkey, an artefact was uncovered by archaeologists. On it was an inscription that read, 'The beginning of the gospel of Caesar Augustus.'[14] The motive behind this message was to announce the news that an emperor had been born who would bring peace to the nations and freedom from oppressors. Therefore, if you pledged allegiance to this leader, you would be saved from destruction and protected from the enemies of the Empire. That sounds like a familiar narrative. Compare the inscription about Augustus to the writer's opening in Mark 1:1, 'The beginning of the good news about Jesus the Messiah, the Son of God.'

In the ancient world, when a nation had achieved a military victory, a runner would carry the good news from the battlelines

---

14 T. Keller, *King's Cross: Understanding the life and death of the Son of God* (London: Hodder & Stoughton, 2011), p. 15.

back to the homeland. The message that these heralds, or 'evangelists' would carry was the gospel, the *euangelion*. They declared good news. Something dramatic had happened that meant the world was different. A battle has been won for you. You are free.

Consequently, the *euangelion* of Jesus Christ is an announcement that something has changed. When we return to Jesus' words in Mark 1, he is announcing that the kingdom of God has come near. He is declaring that through his life, death and resurrection, we are about to see what it looks like when God rules. A King has been born who will bring peace not just to the Roman Empire, but to the cosmos. Freedom is here, not just from earthly armies, but from sin, evil and death. And allegiance to this kingdom is eternal salvation, friendship with the King and a part to play in extending its beautiful borders.

2 A story

One of the things we must learn to do as we mature in faith is hold a number of tensions as Christians. The more we read the Bible, the more these tensions appear – and we must grapple with them accordingly. For example, we grasp hold of the mystery that Jesus was both fully God and fully human. When it comes to how we view God as Father, we must hold onto the fact that he is both personal and powerful. When we consider our own identity, we must grapple with the tension that we are both saints and sinners. We have been made holy already, we are being made holy and we will be made holy. All of these things are true.

And when we consider the gospel, there is another tension to be held. It is both astonishingly simple and profoundly complex. It is so easy to understand that a young child can respond and marvel at it – and so complex that they can grow up and spend a lifetime appreciating its depths.

The late pastor and writer Tim Keller describes it in these terms, 'The gospel has been described as a pool in which a toddler can wade and yet an elephant can swim. It is both simple enough to tell to a child and profound enough for the greatest minds to explore.'[15]

Its complexity is illustrated by the story of a world-famous jazz musician who performed at a club in New Orleans. The audience was mesmerised by her performance and she was invited afterwards to an awestruck press conference. As the cameras flashed and the applause died down, a music journalist cleared his throat, 'That was amazing. Thank you. Can you summarise the essence of your performance in thirty seconds?' The musician turned a shade of beetroot, 'How on earth do you expect me to do that?! I've just played for two and a half hours.' In some ways, when communicating the beauty and breadth of the good news of Jesus, it can feel like we are trying to do something similar. There is a reason the shortest 'Gospel' is sixteen chapters long.

The missiologist David Bosch captures this sentiment like this:

We cannot capture the evangel and package it in four or five 'principles.' There is no universally applicable master plan for evangelism, no definitive list of truths people only have to embrace in order to be saved. We may never limit the gospel to our understanding of God and of salvation.[16]

Hold onto that idea. May you never lose the wonder of how beautiful, majestic, mysterious, far-reaching and profound the gospel is. But while still holding that idea, embrace with us the mandate that as good news people we are to live and proclaim the gospel. In order to do this, we need to find shorter ways of summing up the Christian message. Alongside its complexity, so we can live it

15 T. Keller, 'The Gospel in All Its Forms', Cru, https://www.cru.org/us/en/train-and-grow/share-the-gospel/the-gospel-in-all-its-forms.html (accessed 19 December 2024).

16 D. Bosch, *Transforming Mission: Paradigm shifts in theology of mission* (New York: Orbis, 1991), p. 420.

and tell it, we need simple ways of understanding and encapsulating the essence of the good news.

Fortunately, we are not the first to have embarked on such a task. Over the centuries many people have sought to express the big gospel story in a way that does not offer a comprehensive definition but tries to summarise its heart.

Let's begin with Jesus. There is a reason why John 3:16 has appeared millions of times in billboard print, tattoo ink, social media profiles and gospel tracts. For many, these words from the Son of God capture the heart of the good news:

> For God so loved the world that he gave his one and only Son, that whoever believes in him shall not perish but have eternal life.
> (John 3:16)

From Jesus we move on to Paul. In writing to the church in Corinth, Paul wants to remind the church of 'the gospel' he preached to them.

> Now, brothers and sisters, I want to remind you of the gospel I preached to you, which you received and on which you have taken your stand. By this gospel you are saved, if you hold firmly to the word I preached to you. Otherwise, you have believed in vain.
> For what I received I passed on to you as of first importance: that Christ died for our sins according to the Scriptures, that he was buried, that he was raised on the third day according to the Scriptures, and that he appeared to Cephas, and then to the Twelve.
> (1 Corinthians 15:1–5)

There are more passages we could draw from, of course, but when we ask what is core to the good news, in these two passages alone we see several themes emerging: salvation from death, the sacrifice of Jesus for our sins, the necessity of believing in him, life through the resurrection. When we speak about being gospel people, these are the fibres of our DNA. This is our genetic make-up as evangelicals.

Theologians have crystallised these themes into comprehensive summaries of the gospel. There are many to choose from, but we like this one from N. T. Wright:

> The gospel is the royal announcement that the crucified and risen Jesus, who died for our sins and rose again according to the Scriptures, has been enthroned as the true Lord of the world. When this gospel is preached, God calls people to salvation, out of sheer grace, leading them to repentance and faith in Jesus Christ as their risen Lord.[17]

More technical definitions like this one are useful in some settings, but it is not surprising that as Christians have sought to 'give a reason for the hope that they have' (1 Peter 3:15), they have come up with more memorable and accessible ways of summing up the good news. This quote from C. S. Lewis (though it is often attributed to the Early Church Father and Archbishop of Constantinople, St John of Chrysostom) is a good example: 'The son of God became a man to enable men to become sons of God.'[18]

In recent years, in an evangelistic setting, some people have found tools like The 4 Points to be a useful way of remembering the gospel story.[19] The journey they take you on goes like this:

1 God loves us
2 We have sinned and this separates us from God

---

17 Cited in Bird, *Evangelical Theology*, p. 30.

18 C. S. Lewis, *Mere Christianity* (London: William Collins, 1952), p. 112.

19 The 4 Points, https://www.the4points.com/uk/index.php (accessed 23 October 2024).

3 Jesus died and rose again to save and reunite us
4 We need to make a decision to follow him.

We recognise that this summary has its limitations as a full understanding of the good news – but that is partly because all short summaries will fall short. It is because of the tension we have to hold between simplicity and complexity. Our invitation is to wonder, marvel and live in the vastness and beauty of the gospel story, without ever failing to appreciate it and finding ways to grasp and communicate how simple and compelling it is.

In our efforts to simplify the gospel, we can sometimes reduce its essence to believing a message so that we might gain eternal life. At its worst, we can make the invitation of Christianity into one of joining another religion or lifestyle enhancement. We make it transactional rather than relational. The good news is far better than that.

At its best the gospel is not just about what we have been saved from but who we are saved to. We are saved *from* death, sin and ourselves by the work of Jesus – but we are also saved *to* a living relationship and active apprenticeship to him as well. In him we are set free to become fully human and live as we were created to be, with the Holy Spirit living within us.

The gospel has so much depth to it, and we love discovering more of its beauty. John Stott saw six key aspects of the gospel as noteworthy:

1 The gospel is *Christological.*
2 The gospel is *biblical.*
3 The gospel is *historical.*
4 The gospel is *theological.*
5 The gospel is *apostolic.*
6 The gospel is *personal.*[20]

---

20 J. Stott, *Evangelical Truth* (London: Inter-Varsity Press, 2021), pp. 13–14.

You could fill a theological library looking at just one of these and it is the richness, depth and profound joy of the gospel that has grabbed both of our hearts and lives in the most profound of ways.

3 A person

Like the news that would come back declaring military success, the evangel is a message – but it is not just a message. I, Gavin, was taking part in a radio debate with two secular humanist academics. It was after the pandemic had ended and the morale of the nation was at a particularly low ebb. These two academics spoke first and did nothing but compound the sense of hopelessness in the culture at that moment. I even found myself feeling pulled down by the complete lack of hope that was being put forward and the sense of prevailing doom.

The radio host then turned to me and said, 'Reverend Calver, what do you think about all of this?'

I spoke up and said:

In so many ways, I would love to have the academic ability of these two guys. They have a brain and an intellectual capacity that I will never have. However, all they've done is make me feel worse about the current situation in the UK. For me, hope is not a concept or something 'other'. Hope has a name and his name is Jesus. When you stand on the unchanging one in the midst of the shifting sands of culture, you can hold on to hope. When you know the enduring presence of Jesus, you can get through what's ahead. And having faced all we have these last few years, it's been difficult for all of us, but doing so with Jesus changes everything. Heading forward at this time, I feel profoundly hopeful because I hold on to hope. I hold on to Jesus.

It was live radio and you are not allowed to do a gospel appeal on most radio stations, but as it was live, I had a bit of a go and got halfway through before being cut off! Hope is centred around Jesus. Good news is a person and we cling to him whatever we are facing.

All the definitions of the good news that we have explored centre around him. The gospel story has a central character who can never be extracted from the plot.

Taking it further

- Watch the BibleProject video simply called 'The Gospel' on YouTube.[21] In less than five minutes Tim Mackie and Jon Collins unpack the context and meaning of the biblical words for good news with greater depth than in this chapter.
- Read 1 Corinthians 15:1–11 and reflect on the passage. Take a notepad or a notetaking app on your phone and ask the Holy Spirit to draw your attention to the words. Write down the words that stand out and meditate on their meaning and why they have stood out to you. Ponder afresh how wonderful the gospel is.
- Think for a moment about how you would communicate the good news if someone asked you what Christianity was about at its core. To develop your ability to communicate the gospel to your friends, Chapter 5 of Phil's book, *Story Bearer: How to share your faith with your friends* might help.[22]

Recommended reading

King's Cross: Understanding the life and death of the Son of God by Tim Keller (Hodder & Stoughton: London, 2011) – A masterful unpacking of the major themes of Mark's Gospel, as part of

---

21 Bible Project, 'The Gospel' [Video], YouTube, 12 November 2019, https://www.youtube.com/watch?v=xrzq_X1NNaA (accessed 13 January 2025).

22 P. Knox, *Story Bearer: How to share your faith with your friends* (London: IVP, 2020).

which Keller looks at the meaning of *euangelion* and explores the major themes of salvation and the importance of the cross and resurrection.

Evangelicals: Who they have been, are now and could be, edited by Mark Noll, David Bebbington and George Marsden (Grand Rapids: Eerdmans, 2019) – An American book that is an excellent collection of essays and contributions from numerous, diverse scholars. It contains helpful pieces on the history and background of evangelicalism as well as writings looking at some of the current crisis issues in the USA and the steps forward needed in the days ahead.

The themes of this chapter can be explored further using small group resources, videos and discussion questions. Delve deeper at www.goodnewspeople.church

2

Evangelicals – to the core

Where there is a unified church, the witness to the truth of the gospel is compelling.
Jonathan Lamb[1]

So, we are gospel people, led by a gospel story. But to understand who we are as evangelicals means we need to take one more step along a well-trodden path. We have found it helpful to ask, 'What are the non-negotiable ingredients at the heart of our identity?'

We are not the first to attempt this. Many have sought to crystallise the components of evangelicalism over the years to varying degrees of success. An important contribution was J. I. Packer's work, *The Evangelical Anglican Identity Problem*, which helpfully laid out four claims and six specific convictions.[2] The claims were that evangelicalism is:

1 Practical Christianity.
2 Pure Christianity.
3 Unitive Christianity.
4 Rational Christianity.

He moved on from these general claims to the six specific convictions:

1 The supremacy of Holy Scripture.
2 The majesty of Jesus Christ.

---

1 Lamb, *Essentially One*, p. 38.

2 J. I. Packer, *The Evangelical Anglican Identity Problem* (Oxford: Latimer House, 1978), pp. 15–23.

3 The lordship of the Holy Spirit.
4 The necessity of conversion.
5 The priority of evangelism.
6 The importance of fellowship.

Packer's work on this was profoundly helpful but still remained hard to explain to the everyday Christian in a way that was suitably accessible and concise to maintain their interest. As a result, David Bebbington's wonderful academic historical survey, *Evangelicalism in Modern Britain*, that followed on a decade later, was warmly received and outlined just four clear defining characteristics of good news people. These are the characteristics that we passionately hold to.[3]

Bebbington's quadrilateral

These four facets have become known as Bebbington's quadrilateral; first outlined by him in 1989.[4] When we are asked what an evangelical is, this is where we turn. These salient features are memorable and understandable. His premise was this – evangelicals are:

• Bibliocentric: We believe that the Bible is the inspired word of God and that the Scriptures reveal universal and eternal truth to all humankind.

---

3 As well as the great contributions from Packer and Bebbington, there has been much other helpful work around defining the term 'evangelical'. These include works by Martyn Lloyd-Jones, Michael Green, Alister McGrath and an in-depth work around evangelicalism in the global contexts of Africa, Latin America and Asia included in *The Cambridge Companion to Evangelical Theology* (Cambridge: Cambridge University Press, 2007). Derek Tidball points out that despite the many different writings, Bebbington's quadrilateral is as near to a consensus on what it means to be an evangelical as we could ever hope to reach (D. Tidball, *Who Are the Evangelicals?* (London: Marshall Pickering, 1994), p. 14.

4 D. Bebbington, *Evangelicalism in Modern Britain: A history from the 1730s to the 1980s* (Winchester: Unwin Hyman, 1989), pp. 1–7.

- Cruciocentric: A clear focus on the death and resurrection of Jesus and his atoning work on the cross.
- Conversionist: A strong conviction around the need for personal conversion. People do not come to faith by osmosis. We get on our knees and surrender our lives to Jesus our Saviour.
- Activist: The gospel needs to be lived out in actions too as we seek to make the world more like the kingdom and proclaim God's kingdom come.

Put another way, we believe in the authority of the Bible, the significance of the cross, the need to make a decision and the desire to make a difference. They are a really helpful way of explaining to just about anyone, what it means to be an evangelical. The journalist, Molly Worthen, puts it this way, 'the great virtue of David Bebbington's "quadrilateral" is that it works well with so many different audiences, from academic conferences to cocktail parties.'[5] We will unpack the four facets and explore them one by one.

Bibliocentric

Phil's family often stays in a village on the banks of Loch Fyne in Scotland opposite the picturesque town of Inveraray. For many years, the only amenity was a Post Office that stood next to the cottage where they holidayed. On the shelf behind the counter was a curious artefact: a cigar butt in an otherwise empty jam jar, seemingly worthless. One day, someone asked the Postmistress what it was doing there. It turned out that the cigar butt had belonged to a government official who had passed through the village during the Second World War. Before getting back into his car he had thrown the remains of his cigar on the pavement, where it was picked up and put into a jar by a young girl. That official was

5 M. Worthen, 'Defining Evangelicalism', in Noll, Bebbington and Marsden, *Evangelicals*, p. 171.

Sir Winston Churchill. The cigar had significance because of its source.

As Christians, we get our theology from four main sources: Scripture, tradition, reason and experience.[6] In different expressions of the Church, we find that one of the sources is more important than others. For example, for some people, it is the traditions of the Church that matter, because they provide a sense of continuity and connection to the practices of early Christians. Others emphasise reason, believing that faith must align with rational thought and ethical principles. Experience can be a key source for some, as personal encounters with God shape how they understand and live out their faith.

For evangelicals, there is the clearest of distinctions. The Bible has supreme authority over the others. Australian theologian Michael Bird states, 'Scripture has magisterial authority and is therefore paramount in the quest for spiritual formation and uppermost in the search for theological normativity.'[7] That is not to say that the other sources of theology are unimportant, just that they must always be interpreted through the lens of biblical truth. In many cases and with regard to many issues, the traditional teaching of the Church, cultural norms, and our own experience and worldview may align with Scripture. However, where they do not, it is the Bible that must have the final word and we must amend our perspective and teaching accordingly. This will have an impact on the breadth of our unity as evangelicals. One of Gavin's predecessors, the late Joel Edwards, said that 'evangelicals cannot afford to practise togetherness at the expense of biblical integrity. The tension between unity and truth has ever been an important issue for people who wish to take the Bible seriously.'[8]

---

6 Known as the Wesleyan quadrilateral.

7 Bird, *Evangelical Theology*, p. 52.

8 J. Edwards, *Lord, Make Us One: But not the same!* (London: Hodder & Stoughton, 1999), p. 90.

For every generation, there are issues that arise where Christians are tempted to compromise and accommodate a prevailing worldview. Society is fickle and views on important issues are constantly wavering. One of the benefits and blessings of being a good news person is that it gives us a firm place to stand as others are blown about by the winds of popular opinion. We do not change the Bible to baptise our culture, we want to see our culture transformed by the Bible. We never change the substance of God's truth – but, as Ruth Perrin points out, evangelicalism's 'ability to engage with contemporary culture and adapt to the demands of each subsequent generation are arguably one of its greatest strengths.'[9] We love being part of something that stands uncompromisingly on the Bible but also finds ways to engage the culture we inhabit with this truth in every generation.

For both of us, the Bible has been invaluable as we have grown as disciples of Jesus.

I, Phil, grew up in a household in which if you were to lift the metaphorical floorboards, you would find Scripture permeating the foundations. I would come downstairs each morning to find my parents reading their dog-eared, leather-bound Bibles. I was made to memorise Bible verses in the car on the way to school (a habit I am now inflicting on my sons so it must have had some benefit!). Reading the Bible with a cup of tea in the morning is the first thing I do each day. Over the years, it has been light in the darkest of situations and even having read some passages hundreds of times, they still move me to the core.

For me, Gavin, the Bible has been central to all of my journey following Jesus. The time spent every day with Scripture frames everything else. As someone so naturally activist, I have always done all I can to fight my tendencies to place activity ahead of intimacy. Time spent with Scripture helps keep this balance right

---

9 R. Perrin, *The Bible Reading of Young Evangelicals: An exploration of the ordinary hermeneutics and faith of Generation Y* (Eugene: Pickwick Publications, 2016), p. 6.

for us as Christians. It is so important that we hold to the truth in the pages of the Bible. Many of our brothers and sisters globally are losing life and limb contending for Scripture – those of us in the West must have an equally high view of the Bible. We are often challenged by a Mahatma Gandhi quote about the Bible. He said,

> you Christians look after a document containing enough dynamite to blow all civilisation to pieces, turn the world upside down, and bring peace to a battle-torn planet. But you treat it as though it is nothing more than a piece of literature.'[10]

We find this so challenging and it should serve as an encouragement to us all to centre our lives on Scripture.

I, Gavin, was in southern Sudan many years ago and there was a circle of people under a tree having a meeting in the shade. They came up to our group and asked us through translation if we knew Jesus because they were worshipping him and wanted to invite us to join their group. We did so and for many hours sang in a language we did not understand. I have been at so many Christian conferences and gatherings yet I've never encountered worship as powerful as the worship under the tree that day. After a long time worshipping, their leader spoke to us through translation and said that he'd heard that there was a book about Jesus. He asked if we had ever seen one. It was a mind-blowing moment as we realised that these people were worshipping Jesus in a more intimate and passionate way than we did – and yet they had never seen the Bible. How much more could they know if they could see the book. It gave me a fresh appreciation for Scripture and profound thankfulness for those who had translated it into my tongue many years before.

---

10 T. Alford, *Leadership 101*, Limitless (Elim), https://www.elim.org.uk/Articles/678247/Leadership_Disciplines_12.aspx (accessed 19 December 2024).

We are thrilled at the rapid progress of Bible translation taking place in our day and long to see this enable every tribe and tongue globally to access Scripture in their own language.

Cruciocentric

In looking at the good news as a person in the previous chapter, we established Jesus' centrality at the heart of the gospel and it is no surprise that he is present in this quadrilateral. We are Jesus people. We never want to stop being captivated and amazed by Jesus.

We are both passionate and long-suffering football fans. Every year we look forward with hope and anticipation to the new season and endure cold nights on terraces through the winter – but we ultimately know that it is where you are after the final games that really matter. There is a quote attributed to the former Arsenal manager, Arsene Wenger, whose side was struggling one year during the December fixtures. He said this: 'Christmas is important, but Easter is decisive.' In what was meant to be a press conference about a football match, the Frenchman accidentally made a profoundly true theological statement.

As Christians, we marvel at the incarnation – the fact that the God of the universe became a baby is mind-blowing in its audacity and humility. We delight in the life and teaching of Jesus. We understand our primary calling is to be his disciples. His example and practices give us a way to follow. But for evangelicals, there is particular emphasis on the cross and resurrection. Christmas is important, but Easter is decisive. John Stott writes:

> Evangelical Christians believe that in and through Christ crucified God substituted himself for us and bore our sins, dying in our place the death we deserved to die, in order that we might be restored to his favour and adopted into his family.[11]

11 J. Stott, *The Cross of Christ* (London: Inter-Varsity Press, 2021), p. 7.

This is because we are good news people. At the heart of the good news is our salvation from death and disconnection to life forever and friendship with the living God. The cross and resurrection are absolutely central to how this glorious exchange has taken place. As Paul writes, 'For the message of the cross is foolishness to those who are perishing, but to us who are being saved it is the power of God' (1 Corinthians 1:18).

It's finished.
It's over.
There's more of them than us and they look a lot bigger.
The villain's got the girl and his finger on the trigger.
Voldemort, Sauron and Vader reign.
It's gone to penalties against the Germans again.

It's a terrible feeling when hope is erased,
Faith misplaced,
Virtue defaced,
Gloom embraced,
Reputation replaced with the taste of disgrace.
When you've pushed every door and it's been slammed in your face.
When you realise you're third in a two-horse race.

So come and sit with me on Golgotha's slopes.
See human history at its lowest ebb.
See the forces of goodness and grace on the ropes,
Evil had spoken, last rites read.

In a phoney gown and thorny crown, he's mocked and knocked and shamed.

As he staggers down through an angry town, they spit and
    hit and hate.
Hands that forged galaxies and flung starry trails,
Are pierced and punctured by merciless nails.
His body succumbing to brutal infliction,
These are the horrors of crucifixion.
And as dice are tossed, hope is lost, desolate disciples count
    the cost,
'King of the Jews' his head rest embossed.
A criminal's killing on Calvary's cross.

And as last words cut through foul-smelling air,
The whole of the cosmos cries out in despair.

'It is finished.'
It's over.

But then dawn wakes on Easter day,
Darkness quakes as shadows give way to
The light.

See, resurrection's the plan. It's why God sent him.
And the comeback's on, there's a change of momentum.
The powers of damnation in previous jubilation,
Have been hushed and crushed by the Lord of creation.

He takes the hit, stands where we should have stood.
And that's why we call Friday 'good'.
And he's back with life, with us and blessed.
And that's why we can know it as 'Sunday best'.

So to the four-nil down, to the backs against the wall,
Listen for his rallying, resurgent call.
And to those up against it, in brokenness and pain,
Easter's story roars, 'We go again'.

So, thine be the glory, death's lost its sting.
Here's to Jesus, the comeback king.

'The Comeback' – to see a video of this spoken-word piece performed on location visit www.goodnewspeople.church.[12]

Conversionist

Sir Dave Brailsford is known as the man responsible for revolutionising British Cycling. They had won just one gold medal in the Olympic games in almost 100 years, then under his leadership at the 2008 Olympics, British Cycling won an incredible 60% of the gold medals available. His approach was based on a principle known as the 'aggregation of marginal gains'. The idea is that if you improve by a small margin in lots of areas, those add up to a big change. In a world of self-help and improvement, we can be tempted to think that our spiritual life amounts to just one area of our lives and that if we get that area sorted then that is one more box ticked and we will have slightly better wellbeing.

The decision to become a Christian is not a marginal gain. It doesn't slightly improve our lives. It changes everything. Good news people believe that the most important decision anyone can ever make is to choose to follow Jesus or not. Paul articulates it like this, 'Therefore, if anyone is in Christ, the new creation has come: The old has gone, the new is here!' (2 Corinthians 5:17). When the

12 P. Knox, 'The Comeback', 2020.

prodigal returns, the father exclaims, 'this son of mine was dead and is alive again; he was lost and is found.' (Luke 15:24). John Newton wrote words sung by millions that describe amazing grace that has brought wretchedness to salvation and turned blindness to sight. These are not incremental changes. They are binary states of being. Evangelicals believe that something profound and transformational happens when we repent and believe.

I, Phil, was chatting with a friend who is not yet a Christian who was going through a difficult season in life. Having offered some average advice, not really knowing what else to say and having been friends with this guy for long enough to be so direct I said, 'Mate, I haven't got much more to give you. Genuinely, the best thing you can do is to give your life to Jesus and let him sort it out.' My friend paused and then replied, 'What's the second-best option?'

If today you are reading this and you have decided to surrender your life to Jesus, you have taken the best possible option. Whatever the challenges you face, however hard this chapter in your life is, you have made the most important decision of your life, and you have made it well. If you have not made that choice, it doesn't matter how well your life is going, how much money you have, how happy you are, how successful you have been – you are still living in, at the most, the second-best option for your life.

As we will explore in a later chapter in much greater depth, the aim of evangelism is not just to gain decisions, but to make disciples. Becoming a disciple is a lifelong journey – but it involves key decisions, and none more so than the initial one to repent, believe and commit to becoming a Christian. Marriage is a helpful analogy. A relationship with a spouse requires daily commitment and devotion, but there are key moments of decision along the way – in particular, the decision to get married in the first place.

Just about the best bits of our jobs come on Sunday mornings when we will almost always give people an opportunity to respond to the gospel message and choose to follow Jesus at the end of our talks. Over just the last few years, we have seen hundreds make this their moment to become disciples. Every time it happens, we are overcome with joy. Tears are not far away as we welcome another brother or sister into the family of God.

At one church, I, Phil, noticed a man on the front row earnestly and meekly put his hand in the air to indicate that he had prayed to open his heart to God's invitation of life. After the service, I found out that this was this guy's first time in church, he was homeless and had been banned from local shelters because of anger issues. The church were playing a role in meeting his physical needs and he was meeting the pastor for coffee that week, but he made the most important decision of his discipleship journey that morning.

Since serving as the leader of the Evangelical Alliance, I, Gavin, have found myself challenged time and again to not limit the way in which the Lord wants to lead people to himself. There have been many wonderful moments of seeing people surrender their lives to Jesus on Sunday mornings, at conferences and events, men's curry nights and more, but one particular occasion stands out. It was the first time I found myself preaching into my phone. It was the very beginning of lockdown. I was due to be speaking at one of the main celebrations as part of a conference. I try to give an opportunity for people to follow Jesus as often as possible and that was certainly my original plan when this conference was going to be in person. I'd never preached a gospel message into my phone before, I felt bewildered, not knowing what to do. I couldn't see how a pre-recorded message into my phone would have the same impact, but I felt the Spirit nudge me to preach the sermon with the same passion, the same integrity, the same spiritual preparation, as I would have been doing at the in-person event. I extended my imagination as to what the Lord could do and decided to go for it.

At that stage, I didn't really know how to set up properly so I did the best I could, worked out the ideal settings on my phone and got ready to minister. I worshipped in solitude to the accompanying sounds of some worship videos on YouTube, got myself into the right place to be ready to speak and then preached the message with all the passion I would normally have, despite being in a room on my own. At the end of my talk, I gave a gospel appeal and left time and space for anyone watching to repeat a prayer, after me, surrendering their life to Jesus. It seemed so bizarre and felt so surreal, but I was at least pleased that I'd been faithful and obedient in recording a gospel message with an appeal at the end.

I saved the video and sent it over to the conference for them to use a few days later. Once the online meeting finished, it was really encouraging to receive a number of positive comments and bits of feedback on social media. However, the next day I got a private message on Facebook that was mind-blowing. A woman got in touch with me who had been married for over twenty years to a husband who had no faith at all and very little interest in her relationship with Jesus. Because this gathering had to be on the television she sat in her lounge to join in, and her husband was also in the room but he was reading the newspaper. She felt that he was pretending not to listen at all the whole way through. And yet, when I prayed the prayer to surrender your life to Jesus at the end of the talk, she could not believe what was taking place in her lounge. She found her husband repeating the lines of the prayer after me as he fully surrendered his life to Jesus on their sofa that evening. She was utterly blown away, the prayers of so many years were being answered in that one incredible moment as the tears flowed freely down her face. He had been critical of her faith, shown no interest at all and it was only because this message was being broadcast this way that her husband even heard it in the first place. He would never have gone to the conference in person and it was so encouraging that the Lord moved so powerfully. I came away thinking, 'Wow, Lord, you really can move mountains and do so very much with so little.' Let's not limit the ways in which the Lord wants to lead people to himself. Let's be people who long to see others meet Jesus too through any means possible.

For evangelicals, our passion for conversion arises from our grasp of the gospel. When we understand the goodness of the good news, the necessity of salvation and the invitation to know God, we cannot help but desire that all those around us respond to the message. In New Testament terms, we are bound and obliged in the strongest of terms, 'For Christ's love compels us, because we are convinced that one died for all, and therefore all died' (2 Corinthians 5:14).

When we become captivated by the love of Jesus and its outworking on the cross, we want our world to know its embrace. When we realise the Father's eyes have never left the road down which his child has departed, we want every prodigal to come home. When we are released in the power of the Holy Spirit, who is the chief evangelist, then we can see incredible things take place. The Church is designed to reach out, its birth at Pentecost was a missionary event and we are here to reach others. When we stand and sing of amazing grace, our hearts yearn that our friends sing with us, 'I once was lost but now am found, was blind, but now I see.'[13] We evangelicals are conversion people.

Activist

'It's not fair though, is it?!' remonstrated Phil's young son as they walked through Birmingham city centre as a family. These protestations of unfair treatment were not uncommon for a six-year-old who was working out the boundaries of appropriate behaviour. He had already been on the 'naughty spot' twice that week for crimes against his younger brother. But in this instance,

---

13 J. Wesley, 'Amazing Grace', 1779.

his appeals against injustice were not self-centred. We had just passed a homeless person and Caleb had asked why there was someone sitting by the side of the street in a sleeping bag. We explained that in life, some people have a lot more than others, and some have so little they don't have a bed or a home to sleep in.

Caleb was so affected by that moment as a young boy that for the last five years he has made sure that we financially support the homeless shelter in our city each month as a family. Last time he walked through Birmingham with his dad, he filled his pockets with food to give out on the way. Not to be outdone, his younger brother recently prayed with another homeless person for the first time.

Our final part of the quadrilateral of defining characteristics of evangelicals is that we are activists. Not only does our grasp of the good news lead us to want others to hear about the love and justice of God, but also to experience it in practical ways. We want the world to become more like the kingdom. We don't merely want to see people get into heaven, we want heaven to get into people.

Caleb is a minuscule example of what this has looked like for evangelicals over the centuries. Between 1850 and 1900, as many as three quarters of all voluntary charities were set up and run by evangelical Christians.[14] The evangelical beliefs of the likes of William Wilberforce and Olaudah Equiano were the fire in their hearts and moral compass that inspired and guided their political involvement and activism in seeking to abolish the British slave trade, as well as other faith-fuelled endeavours such as the founding of what became the Royal Society for the Prevention of Cruelty to Animals (RSPCA). The activism of good news Christians and their commitment to human life flourishing led to the creation of healthcare and education institutions often

---

14 K. Heaseman, *Evangelicals in Action: An appraisal of their social work in the Victorian era* (London: Geoffrey Bles, 1962), pp. 13–14.

before others were engaging in them and this continues to this day.

The charity leader, Ben Lindsay, writes of the importance of reflecting God's character as we are activist in our communities.

The church should be presenting the lion as well as the lamb of Jesus' character. People who are struggling to survive day to day need to hear about the God of justice, who will fight on their behalf, as well as the God of grace, who will provide salvation, peace and reconciliation.[15]

As you will see in the next chapter where we explore the history of the Evangelical Alliance, in the UK, good news people over the last century have been at the forefront of community transformation, global poverty relief and standing up to systems of oppression and injustice. The theologian, Amanda Porterfield, points out that the emphasis on the intellectual history of evangelicalism cannot be separated from the importance of understanding that evangelical faith must be lived out in practice too.[16]

Locally and nationally, the Church does an astonishing job to meet the needs of people in the UK. The Church of England recently calculated the financial value they provide to society and found it to be valued at 12.4 billion pounds a year.[17] Combined with other denominations, this amounts to tens of thousands of projects in almost every community across the land. Of the more than 1,600 foodbanks in the UK, a significant proportion are based in church buildings, with over 12,000 churches supporting

---

15 B. Lindsay, *We Need to Talk about Race: Understanding the black experience in white majority churches* (London: SPCK, 2019), p. 134.

16 Noll, Bebbington and Marsden, *Evangelicals*, p. 147.

17 H. Sherwood, 'Churches Tally Up Their Value to Society – at £12.4bn', *The Guardian*, 18 October 2020, https://www.theguardian.com/world/2020/oct/18/churches-tally-up-their-value-to-society-at-124bn (accessed 19 December 2024).

the Trussell Trust network.[18] As the cost-of-living crisis hit, a nationwide initiative began to provide warm spaces for people who were struggling to afford to heat their home. The evaluating research found that the warm space for almost half of beneficiaries was a church building.[19] A 2020 study found that the scale of toddler groups in churches is such that 74% of all parents of under-fives have attended an activity organised by a church group or in a church building in the last twelve months.[20] During the pandemic, we surveyed the member churches of the Evangelical Alliance and found that 88% of them were working to meet the needs of vulnerable people.[21]

So many of our friends are driven by a passion to meet the needs of the last, the least and the lost and address deep injustices in our world. Les Isaac's heart was broken for the young people on the streets of Brixton and he asked what he, as a church leader, could do about their care and safety. As a result, Street Pastors began in 2003. Two decades later, there are over 11,000 trained street pastors in over 240 UK towns and cities who engage with those on the streets at night to care for people, look after those who are vulnerable and make communities safer.

Debra Green founded Redeeming our Communities (ROC) in 2004. ROC facilitates conversations between agencies, churches, schools, police, councillors and residents to respond to needs in a local area. As a result, hundreds of projects have been instigated, involving thousands of volunteers. They range from tackling youth

---

18 R. Farmer, 'Trussell Trust Reports More People Than Ever Using Foodbanks in UK', *Church Times*, 28 April 2023, https://www.churchtimes.co.uk/articles/2023/28-april/news/uk/trussell-trust-reports-more-people-than-ever-using-foodbanks-in-uk (accessed 23 October 2024).

19 Warm Welcome, 'Impact Report 2023–24', https://www.warmwelcome.uk/impact-report (accessed 23 October 2024).

20 'Talking Toddlers', https://www.eauk.org/assets/files/downloads/Talking-Toddlers-Booklet.pdf (accessed 23 October 2024).

21 'Changing Church', https://www.eauk.org/resources/what-we-offer/reports/changing-church (accessed 23 October 2024).

unemployment to mentoring, from clearing unkempt gardens to suicide prevention initiatives.

Christians Against Poverty (CAP) exists to help release people from the cycle of debt and poverty. It was started by John Kirkby who was deeply moved by the crippling financial trap that many fall into. As a result of their intervention, over 20,000 people have become debt free since 2010 and CAP is heralded by many outside the Church as a gold standard of poverty relief, who signpost many to their services. CAP is driven by faith. It is 'the fuel in their engine'. But we are also full of admiration for the way in which sharing the gospel is prioritised alongside debt relief. CAP has not only seen tens of thousands of people released from debt, they have also played a part in more than 8,000 people becoming Christians.

Clearly activism is not limited to evangelicals, or even Christians, but it has always been a hallmark and feature of gospel-centred individuals, churches and organisations. We are good news people, in word and action.

A firm foundation

We hope as you have read these first two chapters, you have been captivated again by the person and story of Jesus. We pray that the theological ground beneath you feels firmer as we enthused and explored the four defining features of good news people. But we also hope that it may have encouraged you to consider what it means to be a gospel-centred blessing to the world around you. We are those who are rooted that we might grow and go.

Our stories – why we are evangelicals

I, Phil, recognise all the characteristics of evangelical faith in my journey as a disciple. My family's story of faith took a significant turn during the Second World War, when my grandfather Neville heard the good news from a chaplain at the RAF base where he was stationed. He returned from duty to share the gospel with all of his family. He then trained in the legal profession, becoming Town Clerk of Harrogate, but also developing a heart and gifting as a preaching evangelist. This combination of law and evangelism has run richly in the DNA of the Knoxes that followed.

Martin was Neville's youngest son. He married Janet and they had three children, of whom I, Phil, am the eldest. My dad was a visionary and hard-working lawyer, specialising in housing and local government law and using it to create better living conditions for those who lived in the poorest areas of the UK. His success brought significant financial reward and responsibility, but his calling to the last and least led him and mum to choose to live on a council estate rather than in a wealthy suburb. This sacrifice and example of faith in action had such a profound impact on my life.

I remember making my first decision to follow Jesus as a six-year-old. I was at a Christian event where someone simply explained the gospel and I responded and invited Jesus into my heart. And the passion I have for others to know God's love started at that early age. At primary school, I persuaded every boy in my class to come to church at one point or another – apart from one, and if you are reading this, Richard Clarkson, we'd love you to get in touch! As a teenager and student, I continued to see myself as a good news person. Tragically, my dad died in 2004, aged 48, and since then my mum in 2020 – but their legacy is a strong and vibrant evangelical faith in each of their children.

After studying law at university, I was praying about my next steps. Through my student years, I had volunteered for Youth for Christ (YFC) and after I graduated, a staff role became available, running evangelistic weekends away for teenagers. Gavin was working for YFC at the time and leading the team that I would be appointed to. The rest, they say, is history, and our friendship and this book are a result of a first conversation in 2005.

I, Gavin, have grown up around evangelicalism throughout my life. There is no escaping the fact that both my late grandfather, Gilbert Kirby, and my father, Clive Calver, led the Evangelical Alliance in previous generations. For all of my life, I have been surrounded by the kind of Christianity that holds firmly to the teaching of the Bible and has a huge passion to reach those around them with the gospel. However, it has not been as simple a journey to his role today as many might guess. It's not like there was a moment when I was small that I was pledged to lead the Evangelical Alliance like a young Simba in the Lion King being promised he would one day be king!

For so many years of my life, I kicked strongly against the Christianity of my family but it was impossible for me to ever doubt the fact that the God who moves mountains continues to do so today. I'd seen so much of the Lord moving around me when I was growing up which meant I could never be in a position to deny the existence of God. The question was always, 'Am I willing to give up everything to follow the Jesus who gave up everything for me?'

When in the early stages of adulthood I surrendered my life to Jesus, it was on the understanding that this was 'full throttle' Christianity without compromise. I threw myself into seeking to reach others with the gospel and promised to go 'wherever, whenever and into whatever' for Jesus. The reason I'm an evangelical Christian is because the Bible drives everything I believe in. The death and resurrection of Jesus is formative to all I hold onto. I have a driving desire to see every person around me come to know the Lord Jesus as their personal Lord and Saviour and I long to see the world become a greater reflection of the kingdom as we live out the kind of activism that changes lives. From a distance, it may appear that this was always where I would end up but in truth there have been many surprises along the way. Every day since my conversion on a park bench in South London, I have been seeking to pass this faith onto others.

Fundamentally, we are both evangelicals because we love Jesus and believe the gospel is true. We are so grateful for the examples of our families and what has been modelled to us in terms of being gospel people and are determined to pass that on to the generations to come. We see in our stories the firm foundations of biblical truth and the sparks that have set our hearts ablaze with a desire to make Jesus known.

Taking it further

- If you have read these chapters and have never understood the good news or responded to God's invitation to follow him, we want to urge you to do so. It really is the best decision you could ever make. If, like the examples in this book, you want to choose to follow Jesus and receive forgiveness for your past, his presence in your present and hope of life forever for your future, we invite you to pray this prayer as a way of accepting his love for you:

Dear Lord, I am sorry where I have got it wrong and gone my own way. Thank you that you love me and in Jesus died and rose again so I could be free from my sin and brokenness, know hope and purpose now, and live forever in heaven. I may not have it all together, but I want to follow you, accept your invitation of life and surrender my life to you. Amen.

- Reflect on the four components of Bebbington's quadrilateral. Which of them make your heart sing the most? Which enthuses you the least? As Gavin and Phil have done at the end of this chapter, reflect on your story and ask yourself where the hallmarks of evangelicalism have played their part in your journey of faith. In a journal, write down your own story of faith and highlight each of these core components of good news people as you do.

- Visit the 'Find an organisation' section on the Evangelical Alliance website.[22] Here you will find over 500 organisations who are part of the membership of the Evangelical Alliance. Take time to appreciate the breadth of work they are involved in to make a difference to people's lives across the UK, as they fulfil the activist characteristic of evangelicalism. Choose a small selection of them and find out more about their work – consider praying for them and supporting their ministry.

Recommended reading

The Cross of Christ by John Stott (IVP: Leicester, 1986) – A classic expounding of why the cross matters and its impact on us as individuals, humanity as a whole and the world. Stott looks at the events at Calvary through a variety of Biblical lenses and explains their relevance to us today.

The Bible: A story that makes sense of life by Andrew Ollerton (Hodder & Stoughton: London, 2020) – A zoomed-out view of the big story of God that gives readers a grasp of the narrative from Genesis to Revelation.

The themes of this chapter can be explored further using small group resources, videos and discussion questions. Delve deeper at www.goodnewspeople.church. There are also resources available here for those who prayed the prayer of commitment to Jesus above.

---

22 'Find an Organisation', Evangelical Alliance, https://www.eauk.org/membership/our-members/find-an-organisation (accessed 19 December 2024).

3

Evangelicals – together making Jesus known

I can do things you cannot, you can do things I cannot;
together we can do great things.
Mother Teresa[1]

One of the craziest, or possibly stupidest, ideas we've ever had was to try and break the world record for the longest ever five-a-side football match. Alongside fourteen other players (there were two squads of eight, with five from each squad playing at any given time), we both attempted this gruelling challenge. But we could not do it alone. So many people contributed towards making this outrageous record attempt even a possibility. A group worked on logistics for the twelve months before the event, the whole thing had to be filmed, food and drink were needed, massages, medical expertise, blister plasters, ice baths – there were so many people helping out and that's before anyone kicked a football. Further still, there were supporters, officials to keep score, referees. The list of those involved seemed endless. Yet, after much pain, anguish, resilience and teamwork, two days after the game had started we had both been involved in setting a new world record of playing five-a-side football non-stop for forty-eight hours, raising £53,000 for Youth for Christ in the process.[2] The score was 900 and something vs 700

---

1 K. Kim, 'Together We Can Do Great Things', Laidlaw Scholars, 22 August 2022, https://laidlawscholars.network/posts/together-we-can-do-great-things (accessed 20 November 2024).

2 For more information on Youth for Christ, visit https://yfc.co.uk. Between us, your authors served at YFC for over twenty-five years and both love the ministry and its

and something, which depressingly means that your authors (on the same team) lost by over 200 goals. A decade on, our egos are still recovering, but we will never forget the feeling of euphoria as the final whistle blew. At this moment, perhaps naturally, all the attention was on the players. But we will always remember that no record would have been broken without the huge team who all worked together in many different roles towards the same target.

It's incredible what is possible when we unite together and people play to their strengths, work hard to help each other, and pursue a common outcome with clear focus. Former President of the USA, Harry S. Truman is credited with saying, 'It is amazing what you can accomplish if you do not care who gets the credit.'[3] How much might be possible for the Church and its mission if we all work as one body and not one of us gets the credit, because Jesus gets it all?

Why evangelical unity

There are many efforts and initiatives that try to gather Christians together for common action and connection. But, we believe the particular merit and beauty of an evangelical foundation gives a compelling common ground which is worth standing on together. When we embrace our identity as good news people there is much mutual blessing and many opportunities to make a difference when we unite with likeminded and like-hearted others.

In this chapter, we will explore what it means to be united and the significance of belonging to a movement that exists to together make Jesus known, in particular, the Evangelical Alliance. It is not the only agent for unity across the whole Church in the UK. But if you, like us, treasure and resonate especially with being good news

---

clear desire to see every young person in Britain come to know Jesus as their personal Lord and Saviour (accessed 23 October 2024).

3 Truman Library Institute, https://www.trumanlibraryinstitute.org/truman/truman-quotes/page/5/ (accessed 20 November 2024).

people, gospel-centred Christians, the Evangelical Alliance is the oldest and largest family of evangelicals and it is for you. We exist for two reasons that have always been at the heart of who we are:

- Unite the Church to reach the lost in every corner of the United Kingdom, and
- Give the Church a clear, united, confident and effective voice into every layer of society.

The movement began from a recognition of the significance of the distinctive points we described in the last chapter and the realisation that there are some things that can only be achieved when we unite around these fundamentals of faith. So that we might understand our togetherness today, we wanted to give you some of the highlights of our history and how we came to be united upon these two aims.

Our keynote is love

The Evangelical Alliance story began on 1 October 1845, when 216 Christian leaders met together in Liverpool's Medical Hall. At this conference, they discussed the core characteristics of biblical foundations, the centrality of Jesus' death and resurrection, the need to choose to follow him and the desire to transform society. There was agreement that these were powerful convictions that could be united around and that a movement of unity was needed. This was combined with a determination that this network of relationships would be defined by what they were *for*, rather than what they were *against*. One quote resounds from the minutes of that gathering in this regard, spoken by Congregationalist John Angell James, 'Every chorus of human voices depends on the "keynote" being rightly struck, and the keynote that must be struck now is love.'[4]

---

4 I. Randall and D. Hilborn, *One Body in Christ: The history and significance of the Evangelical Alliance* (Carlisle: Paternoster, 2001), p. 37.

In true Christian style, a committee was commissioned to discuss a way forward and, less than a year later on 19 August 1846, more than 800 gathered in Covent Garden for a historic moment as the Evangelical Alliance as we know it was born. From the outset, the heartbeat has been for a unity organisation that would 'manifest and promote the unity of Christ's people.'

We enthused in the last chapter about the features and facets of evangelical faith, and these were discussed at length across the days of this inaugural conference, resulting in the creation and adoption of a basis of faith, containing the 'most vital truths' that would provide the ground to stand on and a cause to unite around. Remarkably, these have been largely unaltered over the years that have followed. As evangelicals we agree that doctrine matters. Today, the website page outlining our basis of faith is the most frequently visited page on our site and one of the gifts we have given our members over the years.[5]

Standing up for truth

When we flick back through the pages of the history of the Church as a whole, there are many people and actions of which we can be immensely proud and we can praise God for the faithfulness and courage of those who have graced the chapters before us. Alongside these, there are other episodes that we wish were not there, in which Christians have got things profoundly wrong.

Gladly, in the embryonic days of the Evangelical Alliance, there are some events which cause us to be very grateful and which laid the foundation for a desire to always do the right thing. At its very first conference in 1846, slave ownership was a live issue. At the time, slavery had been abolished in the UK, but emancipation had not taken place in the USA. It was the strong conviction of

---

5 'Basis of Faith', Evangelical Alliance, https://www.eauk.org/about-us/how-we-work/basis-of-faith (accessed 23 October 2024).

some British evangelicals that slave holders should be barred from membership. The minutes from that gathering detail five days of heated exchange, with some moving speeches. Among them was Reverend H. Hinton, the then general secretary of the Baptist Union, who was committed in standing against the evil of slavery. He held to the conviction that those who had slaves must be explicitly prohibited from joining the Alliance.[6] Reverend E. Fraser (referred to in the minutes as 'a gentleman of colour') was a Wesleyan minister from Jamaica who also exhorted the conference to see Christian unity as a key vehicle in combating slavery.[7] This stumbling block was so significant that it prevented the proposed formation of a formally integrated global movement. Instead, each nation would have their own alliance, more loosely affiliated as part of an international network.

It is important to note that debate continued around whether British evangelicals should give up their shares in slave-holding companies. We lament the many failings of the Church in this and other areas – to us today, it is extraordinary that this was even a matter of debate. However, it is clear that, from the start, there has been something in the DNA of the Evangelical Alliance that has sought to be countercultural, stand up for justice and seek to uncompromisingly do the right thing.

A similar test to the integrity and fibre of the Evangelical Alliance came in the 1930s, when Nazism was on the rise in Europe. In 1933, German churches were ordered to display swastikas on their buildings. Many leaders refused and, in defiance, a so-called 'Confessional Church' emerged with over 1,500 pastors reading a declaration against the demands to submit to fascism. The British Evangelical Alliance, under the leadership of Henry Martyn Gooch, stood with the Confessional

---

6 Randall and Hilborn, *One Body*, p. 62.

7 Randall and Hilborn, *One Body*, p. 63.

Church in this act, writing to Hitler and other leaders. The letter stated that events in Germany were, 'a conflict to maintain the principles of the Christian religion.'[8] Alongside this, the Evangelical Alliance advocated on behalf of the persecuted Jews to the British Government, 'to offer the widest possible asylum', to those fleeing Nazi oppression.[9]

A clear and united voice

From the outset we have responded to the mandate, need and call of God to speak truth to power and advocate on behalf of evangelicals from a position of biblical truth. As a result, speaking out on issues that matter has been a core activity of the Evangelical Alliance for virtually all of our existence. Inevitably, when we review the last couple of centuries and consider the events of history and the changes that have taken place in society, there are a great number of complex and contentious issues that we have spoken into. But there are also some common threads, perhaps none more so than freedom of religion and belief. No issue has featured more consistently in the campaigns of our advocacy teams than religious liberty. In the early years especially, this work was as international as it was domestic, speaking on behalf of the religious freedoms of those in Turkey, Russia, Italy and Spain.

But as well as 'evergreen' areas of concern, there have also been 'seasonal' issues that have arisen in the news cycle or societal consciousness, that have warranted a contribution from the Evangelical Alliance. Throughout the twentieth century these have ranged from environmental issues to gambling legislation, from the welfare and justice for those in poverty to sanctity of life issues such as abortion and assisted dying. And in the 1980s and 1990s,

---

8 Randall and Hilborn, *One Body*, p. 176.

9 Randall and Hilborn, *One Body*, p. 177.

dramatic increases in our membership meant that the voice of evangelicals was difficult to ignore.

The number of Evangelical Alliance members influences the strength of the voice when we speak on behalf of the Church on important issues. When you can claim to represent thousands of churches and hundreds of organisations, that is a good start, but increasingly it is the collective voice of individuals that translates into increased political influence. In 1981, the Evangelical Alliance had just 900 personal members. Under the leadership of Gavin's father Clive, an emphasis on membership meant that a decade later this had risen to over 23,000. By 1996, the total surpassed 50,000. This growth coincided with more and more opportunities to speak into public policy, with good news being heard and Clive and his team regularly meeting key political leaders and speaking on behalf of Christians in the media and corridors of power.

Navigating theological issues

One of the first theological issues that the newly formed Evangelical Alliance had to negotiate was that of Darwinism and evolution. Charles Darwin's *On the Origin of Species* was published in 1859 and for some evangelicals, it represented a challenge to a traditional view of how the world was created. As you may imagine, some evangelicals arose in staunch opposition to the theory, while others maintained that science and faith were not enemies, but friends.

Professor James McCosh was a keen supporter of the Evangelical Alliance and he helped the membership overcome initial caution around these potentially threatening ideas. He encouraged the exploration of an assimilation between God's intricate design of the world and Darwin's natural law. He maintained that humankind had been created as a distinct species, but that the development of life across other species could have evolved as Darwin observed, and that these adaptations were part of the Creator's masterplan.

Moreover, they pointed towards the majesty and creativity of a God, who has engineered 'an evidently contemplated end, in which are displayed the highest wisdom and the most considerable goodness.'[10] Clearly this debate has continued and evangelicals have consistently found common ground on a biblical 'why' of creation, while reasoning around the 'how' and 'when' and reaching different conclusions.

And wherever you land on this issue, this episode is a useful starting point for us as evangelicals when we begin to ask the question of where we should draw the lines on significant, contentious issues of theology and culture. As we have also seen in the case of slave owners and the rise of Nazism – and will continue to see in the challenges that emerge in the twentieth and twenty-first centuries – we have taken each issue at a time. There are some that need confronting head on, with an unwavering stance, and others which require a more nuanced response. With both, great wisdom is needed – to know when to engage, how to apply Scripture and to get the tone of communication right. We will continue to explore these themes in the chapters ahead.

The response to evolutionary theory marked the first occasion that the Evangelical Alliance felt the need to address a challenge coming from outside the Church. Other concerns emerge from within the evangelical family and over the decades we have spoken into issues surrounding the nature of hell, the authority of Scripture, revivalism and the 'Toronto Blessing', and many more. Two things are important to note.

First, the role and posture of the Evangelical Alliance have been important in these instances. As we will explore further in Chapter 8, to be an evangelical is to recognise that no one stream or denomination can do it by themselves – and there are a number of issues that the different streams will disagree on. The key question

---

10 J. McCosh, *Christianity and Positivism: A series of lectures to the Times on natural theology and Christian apologetics* (London: McMillan, 1871), p. 92.

is which issues are primary and which are secondary. Primary issues will define the parameters of evangelical doctrine and would be the so-called 'hills to die on'. Our certainty on these comes from a clear understanding of what the Bible says on these matters. Secondary issues would be those on which the Bible allows some diversity of belief and practice.

The early years of the Alliance set the tone for where to draw the boundaries, as Ian Randall and David Hilborn articulate:

> The Alliance was quick to condemn modern rationalist and secular thinking when it appeared to threaten the gospel, and organised various committees, campaigns and rallies to counter this threat. Typically, however, it maintained a generous stance on the 'right to private judgment' and eschewed the more separatist and reactionary doctrinal structures of what would come to be known as fundamentalism.[11]

Secondly, as good news people, we can take great heart from our history. As we have navigated complex and weighty issues in our past, we can face the challenges of the future with confidence. The same God that gave wisdom to those facing new scientific discovery, global conflict, rapid technological development, dramatic shifts in cultural worldview and controversial theological assertions in the past is the same God who will help us face whatever is to come. Every generation has its battles. The challenges to biblical truth today feel monumental to so many of us, just as they would have done to our forerunners, but the history books in the years ahead will look back on this era as one where we continued to hold firm to our gospel convictions. God has seen us through before and will do so again, whatever the future holds.

---

11 Randall and Hilborn, *One Body*, p. 133.

At our best on the front foot – making Jesus known

In the preceding chapters, we emphasised the need for us as evangelicals to have a firm theological place to stand and a gospel-shaped ambition to see people's lives transformed by Jesus. For the Evangelical Alliance, the evangelistic and missional genes that were present in the 1846 convention have been reproduced in the cells of activity in the initiatives that followed. The core passage of Scripture at that conference was John 17, where Jesus' prayer for unity has a purpose and a consequence, 'so that the world will know' (verse 23). Our deep desire as gospel people is nothing short of revival. We are captivated by the vision that every heart and soul – in every community and in every layer of society – hears, responds to and lives out the good news of Jesus.

As we track this theme through the Evangelical Alliance's history, a number of highlights emerge. A prominent evangelistic approach in the nineteenth and twentieth centuries involved invitations to mass rallies for people to hear a celebrated preacher. To gather large numbers of listeners would take an interdenominational unity movement with a heart for the gospel – thus emerged the Evangelical Alliance for such a time as this. From as early as 1857 and a revival in Tyneside, we were at the heart of bringing the Church together so that people might hear the good news. In 1873, the evangelists D. L. Moody and Ira Sankey visited Britain from America, supported by the Evangelical Alliance. The leaders of the Welsh Revival of 1904–5 received similar support. In 1924, we organised large-scale evangelistic presentations as part of the British Empire Exhibition at Wembley. And it would be the partnership between the Evangelical Alliance and another American that would take our reputation for evangelism to the next level.

The most listened-to evangelist of the twentieth century was the American Billy Graham. He preached globally to an estimated lifetime audience of 2.2 billion people, many at live events.[12] His first visit to Britain came in 1946 with Youth for Christ (YFC). British YFC was founded as a result a year later. At their conference in 1948, Dr Graham established his first contact with the Evangelical Alliance and plans for a sizeable outreach campaign in the 1950s began. An organising committee was formed, large meetings of church leaders were held, but no one was prepared to put forward the money to make it happen.

The team at the Evangelical Alliance was so convinced of the need for the tour that they put up the entirety of the funds themselves, committing all of their reserves. It was a decision that would cripple them financially and you can imagine the nervousness before the doors opened on the first night as the organisers stared at 15,000 empty seats in the Harringay Arena in prayerful anticipation. And yet, hours later, every seat was taken. And they returned night after night. The initial plan was to run for four weeks. Three months later after audiences in Hyde Park and Trafalgar Square, the crusade ended in front of a crowd of 120,000 people at Wembley Stadium. The cumulative audience totalled over two million, with over 38,000 recorded people committing to follow Jesus in response to the gospel message. Dr Graham also met Sir Winston Churchill and preached in the chapel at Windsor Castle in the presence of Her Majesty Queen Elizabeth II.[13]

These gatherings are still referred to by thousands of Christians as important moments in their faith journeys and stories of conversion. The Evangelical Alliance finances recovered. The combination of our passion to unite the Church around the gospel and its reach across thousands of churches and organisations made this partnership crucial to the success of the large-scale events. It

---

12 'Billy Graham's Life and Ministry by the Numbers', Lifeway Research, 21 February 2018, https://research.lifeway.com/2018/02/21/billy-grahams-life-ministry-by-the-numbers/ (accessed 19 December 2024).

13 'Harringay Crusade', Evangelical Alliance, https://www.eauk.org/church/billy-graham/harringay-crusade.cfm (accessed 23 October 2024).

is also thought that these months in the UK also had an impact on Billy Graham, resulting in a widening of his horizons beyond the USA, with many international visits following this one. These times also led to relationships being formed with the likes of John Stott, which in turn led to the eventual birth of the Lausanne Movement.[14]

Throughout the decades that followed, the Evangelical Alliance has continued to support, galvanise and inspire evangelism in a multitude of ways, uniting the Church around missional initiatives, equipping individuals to share their faith and reminding evangelicals of the supreme importance of the good news story to live and tell. In recent years, we have pioneered an online portal, which has told stories of people having recently come to faith, provided a menu of resources from member organisations for churches and individuals to engage in mission, and established a multi-author blog on best practice in this area.[15] We have also done more to equip and inspire Christians to share their faith and be good news in whatever environment or context God has placed them in.[16]

Word and deed

In the last chapter, we highlighted activism as a salient feature of good news people. As we track the value of evangelicalism through our history, we see again the birth of a number of significant projects.

1959 was 'World Refugee Year' and the Evangelical Alliance started a fund to help contribute to meet the needs of people groups

---

14 The Lausanne Movement (https://lausanne.org) held their first Lausanne Congress in 1974 to seek to help catalyse global evangelisation. It recently held its fourth congress in Seoul in 2024 (accessed 23 October 2024).

15 'Great Commission', Evangelical Alliance, https://www.eauk.org/great-commission (accessed 23 October 2024).

16 'Public Leadership', Evangelical Alliance, https://www.eauk.org/what-we-do/initiatives/public-leadership (accessed 23 October 2024).

who had been displaced by war or disaster. Over the following years, it was decided that the purposes of this fund should be broadened to include wider relief work and that beneficiaries could be all those affected by extreme poverty. The embryonic fund had been nurtured under the leadership of Gavin's grandfather, Gilbert Kirby.[17] The theology of his successor as general secretary of the Evangelical Alliance, Morgan Derham, encapsulated gospel living in both word and action and the opportunity to make a difference to the poorest in our world. He also sensed the need for a specifically evangelical aid charity for people to give to.

> Derham was convinced that the Fund had potential. Evangelicals, he felt, were waking up to their social responsibilities. At the same time he was concerned to remove what he called 'the evangelical alibi' for non-nvolvement in relief schemes, namely that there were no evangelical bodies through whom money could be given and care expressed.[18]

This pot of money was eventually given a name: The Evangelical Alliance Relief Fund. When abbreviated, this became Tearfund. Today, Tearfund is one of the largest relief and development agencies in the UK, with an annual income of over £85 million, working in more than fifty countries responding to disasters and conflicts and partnering with churches to help communities to lift themselves out of poverty. This is how it started.

One of the important themes of our advocacy work has been to speak up on behalf of the poorest in our society. A major 1997 report commissioned by the Evangelical Alliance entitled 'Surveying the Roots of Social Breakdown' highlighted not only

---

17 Obituary, 'Gilbert Kirby: Evangelical pastor and principal of the London Bible College', *The Times*, 3 November 2006, https://www.thetimes.com/article/gilbert-kirby-k2nf0vtssz7 (accessed 23 October 2024).

18 T. Chester, *Awakening to a World of Need: Recovery of Evangelical social concern* (Leicester: IVP, 1993), p. 42.

the needs of over 44,000 people affected by homelessness, poverty, addiction, crime and family breakdown, but what the Church was doing to help provide solutions. As a result, all the major political parties approached the 2001 General Election 'seriously addressing the issue of "faith-based welfare" and government support for church social projects.'[19]

In 2011, the acute and growing need for foster carers and adoptive parents was filling our newsfeeds. Krish Kandiah, who was part of the leadership team at the Evangelical Alliance, gathered partners from Thirtyone:eight and Care for the Family to run a campaign and raise the profile of fostering and adoption and inspire Christians to join in and play their part. Just three years later, in 2014, Home for Good became a charity and today makes a difference in the lives of thousands of children and young people.[20]

These issues remain important to UK evangelicals. In the build-up to the 2024 General Election, we asked our membership what the most important political issues were to them. The top two chief concerns were the economy and poverty.[21]

Stream of streams

One of the incredible joys of working at the Evangelical Alliance is the fact that we're actually a stream of streams. What this means is there are many different parts of the Church coming together as one through the umbrella that is the Evangelical Alliance. There are over eighty different networks, streams or denominations within our membership and it is such a joy to work across these places. Some have characterised our purpose and passion in this area as a 'bringing together of the tribes'. In an increasingly tribalistic

19 Randall and Hilborn, *One Body*, p. 348.

20 Home for Good, https://homeforgood.org.uk (accessed 20 November 2024).

21 'Thinking Faithfully about Politics', Evangelical Alliance, https://www.eauk.org/general-election/thinking-faithfully-about-politics (accessed 23 October 2024).

world, we like this description. Each tribe holds its distinctiveness but unites around the gospel and a shared desire to see kingdom territory expand. Where others might see boundaries, we see the opportunity to move forward together as one.

We love the breadth that makes up the Evangelical Alliance. We want to serve gatherings from New Wine to Keswick; church streams from the Fellowship of Independent Evangelical Churches (FIEC) to the Redeemed Christian Church of God (RCCG); organisations which range in size from a few in a lounge to thousands in the largest of auditoriums; ministries serving age groups from the cradle to the grave; those working with the homeless through to those serving in a palace. We are here for the full breadth of UK evangelicalism.

It does make Sunday mornings interesting. When we go to speak somewhere, we're never quite sure of the type of place we're in until the first worship song starts! The name of the church tells you something but, in reality, the way the visit plays out keeps us on our toes. It means that we may go into rooms where we are with people who long to see the same things but express that quite differently stylistically, tactically or in other ways. I, Gavin, remember a significant conversation with my predecessor as leader of the Evangelical Alliance, Steve Clifford, in my first week on staff. I was Director of Mission and Steve said to me, 'You're one of the most competitive people I've met.' In the moment I wasn't sure if it was a compliment or a piece of criticism until Steve said, 'We don't compete here with one another. We compete against the darkness, alongside all of the light. If a part of the Church does well or sees significant breakthrough, then we celebrate. If an organisation in our membership is thriving, we cheer them on.' This was such a helpful moment. When I had served at Youth for Christ, the temptation was to make sure that everything served YFC and our ends. However, at the Evangelical Alliance we get the privilege of cheering on the Church, shouting loudly about the Church and supporting anything going well. This is a real joy. It allows us to amplify what is happening and means that when we engage with the government, other corridors of power and places of influence, we get to speak on behalf of many parts of the Church, not just one stream. We love being part of a stream of streams and will continue to do all we can to serve widely moving forward.

That is the story and family of which you are a part as a good news person. On our journey through these opening chapters, we hope that you have felt a deeper connection to your identity as a Bible-centred, cross-shaped, new-created agent of change. We pray that you will have looked back at the grand narrative you are part of and see afresh your part in today's God-given moment. And may you also have glimpsed a snapshot of the UK-wide community of evangelicals you are a part of as we together make Jesus known. From this platform we invite you to ponder your posture...

Taking it further

- If you have been inspired by the past and present of the Evangelical Alliance and are not yet a personal member, would you join us? By doing so, you are increasing the size of our membership and consequently the strength of our voice as good news people in the corridors of power. You are also playing your part in helping equip and inspire the Church to make Jesus known. To join today costs just £3 a month and if you are part of a couple, please join together – it is still £3 a month and counts as two. Become part of us here: www.goodnewspeople. church/join

- If you are interested in a much deeper dive into the history, breadth and depth of the Evangelical Alliance, read *One Body in Christ*. Written in 2001, Ian Randall and David Hilborn's work is detailed and comprehensive and contains many of the historical primary sources from the archives. The whole book can be viewed and read for free at www.goodnewspeople.church/onebodyinchrist

- Visit the 'Find a Church' page on the Evangelical Alliance website.[22] Type your postcode in and explore where the Evangelical Alliance member churches are near you. Take a look at the number and diversity of congregations represented. If your church is not yet a member, consider asking the leader(s) to explore joining us. Our encouragement is to deeply love your postcode, while being connected nationally.

Recommended reading

One Body in Christ: The history and significance of the Evangelical Alliance by Ian Randall and David Hilborn (Carlisle: Paternoster, 2001) – A thorough look at the history of the people, events and places that have made the Evangelical Alliance what it is today.

Healing the Divides: How every Christian can advance God's vision for racial unity and justice by Jason Roach and Jessamin Birdsall (Epsom: The Good Book Company, 2022) – A biblical exploration of the racial divisions in our nation and how we can respond well as Christians. In understanding the current conversation around intercultural unity, this book helps us see the perspective of many within the diverse communities across the church and beyond.

The themes of this chapter can be explored further using small group resources, videos and discussion questions. Delve deeper at www.goodnewspeople.church

---

22 'Find an Evangelical Alliance Member Church', Evangelical Alliance, https://www.eauk.org/churches.

Selah

We began this book by describing our need for a firm place to stand and a compelling vision to captivate us. We hope that as we have described the goodness of the good news and the story we are part of, you have felt your footing strengthened and your vista expanded. We stand on the Rock of Ages and on the shoulders of giants.

At this point in the journey, we are going to change tack. If Part 1 articulated where we stand, Part 2 will consider how we stand. Where Part 1 explained what we believe, Part 2 will ask how we live it out. In Part 1 we mostly looked back, in Part 2 we will look forward.

The way we hold ourselves matters. We have identified five postures that we believe are crucial for how we live in this season:

- We need to be brave and kind
- We need to be culturally relevant without selling out
- We need to be hopeful and realistic
- We need to go for decisions and make disciples
- We need to be united and diverse

Some relate more to us as a whole Church rather than individuals, and vice versa. Amidst rapid cultural and technological change, and as those around us are deprived of hope and grow increasingly spiritually hungry, we believe these five postures will characterise what good news people will look like in a bad news world.

In one way or another, within each posture, there is a tension. We are going to invite you to be brave *and* kind, be culturally relevant *without* selling out, be hopeful *and* realistic, go for decisions *and* make disciples, and be united *while* celebrating diversity. None of these requires a binary choice, and some are easier to navigate than others, but we are going to ask you to resist living at the extremes of each scale and allow each value to balance the other.

In each of the following chapters, we will also share stories from our experiences over recent years in the UK Church. We hope the life, diversity and beauty of each will encourage you. We pray that they will help paint a picture of the story you are part of and inspire you that the King is on the move.

Before we begin, our invitation is to pause, close your eyes and take a breath. In the Bible's songbook, the Psalmists punctuate their works with pauses, known as a *selah*. Before we move on to look at the posture of our hearts and lives, take a moment to ask the Spirit of God to examine you and open yourself up to be challenged, encouraged, fired up and changed.

Search me, God, and know my heart;
    test me and know my anxious thoughts.
See if there is any offensive way in me,
    and lead me in the way everlasting.
(Psalm 139:23–4)

Part 2

HOW SHOULD WE LIVE?

4

We need to be brave and kind

Being brave isn't the absence of fear. Being brave is having that
fear but finding a way through it.
Bear Grylls[1]

A single act of kindness throws out roots in all directions, and
the roots spring up and make new trees.
Amelia Earheart[2]

Both of our summers are often spent visiting and speaking at
numerous conferences and events. The summer before being
appointed to lead the Evangelical Alliance, I, Gavin was travelling
as normal and enjoying seeing the Lord move powerfully. Exciting
though the conference season is, it is also incredibly tiring and it
takes a lot to go from place to place and give it your all. Having
been all over the UK, my last stop was the familiar place of Shepton
Mallet for the New Wine summer conference. There was one
specific meeting where I was not ministering and I greatly enjoyed
sitting there and having the chance to receive great teaching
and ministry in the warmth of a friendly crowd. After a time of
powerful worship, the preacher got up and spoke passionately about
the need for the Church to rise up in our day and be the salt and
light culture-shapers that the UK required. At the end of the talk,
the speaker gave a call for anyone feeling challenged about the need
to be distinct for Christ in our secular landscape to make their way

---

1 Quote attributed to Bear Grylls.
2 Random Acts of Kindness, https://www.randomactsofkindness.org/kindness-quotes/
132-a-single-act-of-kindness (accessed 23 October 2024).

to the front. I immediately shot out of my seat and went forward. I knew this call was for me and as I stood at the front of this large tent I felt the Lord challenge me to be braver for him in the next chapter of my life.

'But aren't I already brave for you, Lord?' I found myself desperately crying out. Despite my best attempts to get out of it, the Lord was speaking and I eventually yielded to him and accepted that greater bravery was what was needed. As I stood there at the front of the tent surrounded by thousands of other Christians, I felt myself slowly facing up to the reality of what it might actually mean to be brave. What might it cost? Where might it take me? How would I keep going? What would it mean for my family? As these thoughts flooded through my mind, I felt myself begin to weep. Not cry a little – really weep. The tears poured freely as I surrendered fully to what the Lord might be calling me into.

So often we assume that bravery involves no fear and is easy for some. It is not. People are not born brave – they are given an opportunity to be brave. Bravery is developed in us, not handed out at birth to a select few. From the heroes of the Old Testament to the early believers, Scripture is full of examples of those who were brave when they were given the opportunity to be. The 32nd President of the USA, Franklin D. Roosevelt, said that 'Courage is not the absence of fear, but rather the assessment that something else is more important than fear.'[3] For so many of us, it's a case of not letting our fears be the end of the story but allowing our bravery and courage to help us see beyond the fear and go for it. I wiped my face and went to tell my wife Anne about this encounter.

Some weeks later, on the last night of the summer holidays, we were sitting around having a family meal. Once we had finished

---

3 C. Killick, 'Courage Is Not without Fear', Making Teams Work, 27 April 2020, https://makingteamswork.co/2020/04/27/courage-is-not-without-fear/ (accessed 20 November 2024).

eating, we reflected on the great memories we had made and prepared for a return to normality with a new academic year to get on with. The conversation turned into prayer followed by a time of silence to see if the Lord wanted to say anything to the family. In the Calver home, we try and 'wait' regularly because we are desperate for our kids to learn that prayer is a conversation and not a monologue. After a minute or so in silence, my daughter Amelie spoke up, knowing nothing of my encounter at the front of that tent. A little tentatively she said, 'Dad, it's a bit weird but I think Jesus wants you to be braver going forward.' What incredible confirmation. I sat there completely taken aback but also prepared to hear what the Lord was saying loudly and clearly to me.

Fast forward to today and I find myself leading the Evangelical Alliance. The role is certainly a real privilege, but it also explains why the Lord had been showing me that I needed to be braver. There are so many challenges around us and it is so important that we are prepared to be different – to be influencers rather than the influenced – in the face of a rampant secular agenda. There are moments where both of us find ourselves in situations of influence needing to speak up. We get to take the voice of UK evangelicals into places like the parliaments across the UK, into Scotland Yard, secular media environments and Downing Street. In these settings, an extra level of bravery is required as we seek to speak truth to power. As I find myself preparing to enter such spaces, I will often sing this old chorus to myself:

Turn your eyes upon Jesus.
Look full in His wonderful face.
And the things of earth will grow strangely dim,
in the light of His glory and grace.[4]

---

4 G. Romanacce, K. Winebarger, N. Stiff and N. Trout, 'Turn Your Eyes', Sovereign Grace Music, https://sovereigngracemusic.com/music/songs/turn-your-eyes/ (accessed 23 October 2024).

It is so important that, as we are brave, we are also reminded of the perspective of heaven and the enduring presence of the Lord. With him alongside us, it becomes easier to stand firm on biblical teaching, speak up within the corridors of power on behalf of the UK Evangelical Church and reach out to those around us with a message of hope that can only be found in the gospel.

For us evangelicals, this next decade is going to be really significant as we face up to the increasingly choppy waters ahead of us. We must stand firm on Scripture in a time of incredible challenge, both culturally and spiritually. We need to be prepared to be distinct, despite the overwhelming pressure to conform coming from the secular tsunami taking place in our culture. These winds and waves require a brave posture from us. In this, great heart can be taken from the pages of church history where generations of Christians were able to see great things, and not lose their confidence, despite a very challenging cultural narrative. This is seen in Mary the mother of Jesus. The New Testament professor, Esau McCaulley, says that 'the testimony of Mary is that even in the shadow of the empire there is space for hope and that sometimes in that space, God calls us from the shadows to join him in his great work of salvation and liberation.'[5]

But as well as being braver, we must make sure that we are also kinder. Bravery and kindness are not mutually exclusive. Indeed, bravery without kindness risks being right without relationship. At our worst, we evangelicals have stood up for the truth in a way that diminishes, dismisses or even tramples on others. Our posture matters. You can be brave in righteous belief, while being kind and winsome in how and when you communicate it. And these characteristics are mandated by our evangelical identity. They are found repeatedly in the pages of the Bible and in the person of Jesus.

And kindness is so beautiful. In Charlie Mackesy's bestseller, *The*

---

5 E. McCaulley, *Reading While Black: African American Biblical interpretation as an exercise in hope* (Downers Grove: IVP Academic, 2020), p. 89.

Boy, the Fox, the Mole and the Horse, the characters debate what is better than cake or a hug. This is the Horse's conclusion, 'Nothing beats kindness… it sits quietly beyond all things.'[6] A few years ago, I, Phil, and my wife Dani were in the middle of a particularly tough season of life. We had a young family, I was managing a demanding project at work and we were exhausted, stretched and running on fumes. Desperate to steal some time together away from life's 'trenches', some friends agreed to babysit and we ventured out for a meal. In our keenness, we arrived at the restaurant half an hour early so they sent us away to get a drink until our table became available, but did so with these words, 'Come back at 7:30 but just so you know, we received a phone call today and your bill tonight will be covered.' We looked at each other in disbelief, close to tears. We will always remember how good the food tasted as our souls caught up with one another that night. But we will also never forget how it felt to be recipients of such exquisite kindness.

I, Gavin, remember the excitement in my household when my wife Anne, our young daughter Amelie and I were due to be heading to America to see our family for the festival of Thanksgiving. The car was packed full to leave for a really early morning flight and we were just heading to bed when Anne realised she was bleeding. She was pregnant with our second child and we suddenly didn't know what to do. Our plane was due to take off in a matter of hours and we were thrown into a real sense of desperation. We rang the NHS and were told in no uncertain terms that the idea of flying anywhere was impossible.

Instead of flying to the other side of the world, we drove to hospital in our car packed full of suitcases praying that everything would be OK. An ultrasound scan revealed that though our baby was still in the womb it no longer had a heartbeat. Our child had died. In a matter of hours, our whole world was thrown into great

---

6 C. Mackesy, *The Boy, the Mole, the Fox and the Horse* (London: Ebury, 2019).

confusion. We felt so hopeless and were grieving for a baby we would now never meet. Anne was told she would need to come back the next day for a medical process to remove the baby from her body and so we headed home broken, isolated and desperate.

Not long after our return home, a number of our friends turned up on the doorstep. They had the food shopping needed to replenish our empty fridge, helped us to unpack everything we had prepared to take away with us, and prayed and cried with us as we faced up to what we were going through. They showed up for us in our moment of great pain. Sometimes kindness is what we really need – and what others are crying out for from us too. We will never forget the kindness and compassion we were shown that day.

Another clear example of kindness for Gavin comes from one of his oldest friends. This friend and Gavin disagree on many things, and there have been times when Gavin has publicly expressed views that his friend strongly opposes and which are in sharp contrast to the way he lives. However, this particular friend is often the first to ring Gavin and check he is OK, to be in touch to see if he is coping with a social media onslaught or a challenging week. Being kind does not mean always agreeing with someone's decisions or opinions, but we do need to stand with them in the situations they are facing.

In being kinder, we need to be more courageous and loving, more biblical and compassionate – not treating people as objects but, instead, disagreeing well and without prejudice. Evangelicals sometimes have a poor record in showing love and kindness to those who disagree with them. We must not be foolhardy in our bravery but treat everyone with the dignity that they deserve as someone that Jesus died for.

Because we are created differently, our personality types mean that most of us find that either bravery or kindness comes more naturally to us. But these traits must go together. Apart from Jesus (!), the best example we can think of in the Bible is from the

Christmas story when Joseph, somewhat understandably, intends to divorce Mary. After all, he's just heard that she is pregnant and he is not the father. They are not married but they are betrothed and, in that day, the breaking of an engagement was a legal matter. Genuinely believing that his betrothed has been unfaithful to him, Joseph decides to do what he feels is right – and he plans to divorce her. However, he does not want to hurt and humiliate her, he wants to be kind. So he sets out to do it away from the crowds and with as much love as possible. This seems to us to be what it means to be both brave and kind. Doing the right thing but acting with compassion as you do it. Treating people the right way and loving them, while not losing truth. Also, like Joseph, we want to be up for a complete change of direction in the light of an angelic visitation![7]

So, as we look out on an increasingly challenging landscape, let's be praying for one another, standing together, remaining hopeful as we long to see many people come to faith in Jesus. Perhaps it's time for us all to be a little braver... and kinder.

The brave and kind posture has implications for both how we stand firm and how we share our faith. First, let us consider how being brave *and* kind guides how we stand up for truth.

Brave in standing firm

There is a famous study on peer pressure known as the Asch conformity experiments. Participants were given a simple perception test, where they were handed two cards. One had a single line on it. The other had three lines of differing lengths on it, labelled A, B and C. The line on the first card matched the length of a line on the second card and participants had to say aloud the correct letter corresponding to that line. It was so straightforward that, under normal circumstances, correct responses were expected

---

7 G. Calver and A. Calver, *Unleashed: The Acts church today* (London: IVP, 2020), p. 32.

almost 100% of the time, as demonstrated by a control group. However, there was a twist. Seven out of the eight participants were actors and they were primed to all give, and say aloud, the same wrong answer. The experiment was about testing how likely people are to give into peer pressure and conform, even if the truth is obvious.

Startlingly, over a third of participants followed the others and gave the wrong answer. It prompted lead researcher Solomon Asch to conclude, 'That intelligent, well-meaning young people are willing to call white black is a matter of concern.'[8] Such a summary reminds us of the apt biblical comparison that we are like sheep in need of a shepherd. Yet the need for a shepherd becomes more desperate when society views change at breakneck speed. Prevailing worldviews have shifted dramatically on important issues. In a whirlwind of national campaigns and social media influencers, millions are swept along in a herd mentality.

Throughout the history of the Church, there has been an ever-present pressure to culturally conform and compromise our convictions. Polish painter Henryk Siemiradzki's work, *Candlesticks of Christianity*, depicts first-century believers being smeared in pitch and used as torches in the Roman Emperor Nero's garden.[9] Historian Tom Holland describes the martyring of our forefathers when they were savaged by dogs, lashed to crosses and set alight.[10] Others were gored by bulls or roasted on red hot chairs of iron. This hellish torture could have been evaded if only

---

8 S. E. Asch, 'Effects of Group Pressure upon the Modification and Distortion of Judgments', in H. Guetzkow (ed.), *Groups, Leadership and Men: Research in human relations* (Carnegie Press, 1951), pp. 177–90, https://psycnet.apa.org/record/1952-00803-001 (accessed 23 October 2024).

9 'File: Henryk Siemiradzki – Candlesticks of Christianity, sketch – MP 2040 MNW – National Museum in Warsaw.jpg', Wikimedia Commons, https://commons.wikimedia.org/wiki/File:Henryk_Siemiradzki_-_Candlesticks_of_Christianity,_sketch_-_MP_2040_MNW_-_National_Museum_in_Warsaw.jpg (accessed 23 October 2024).

10 T. Holland, *Dominion: The making of the Western mind* (London: Little, Brown, 2019), p. 83.

they had conformed and bowed the knee to Caesar as Lord. Today, millions of Christians face a similar daily choice in nations where the authorities are hostile to those who profess his name.

Most of us are not under this level of intense persecution. The form it takes is perhaps more subtle. Our marginalisation happens as we are encouraged to 'leave our faith out of it,' or at the very least seen as a bit odd. The comedian, Frank Skinner, puts it this way in his autobiography; 'In a society where all manner of once smirked upon behaviour like wearing crystals and Feng Shui has become acceptable, only Christian belief can definitely guarantee you the label "weird".'[11] The threat of being labelled like this can tempt us to conform to a worldly view.

On what issues might we need to be brave? What are the circumstances that require great courage? The first we see is around the uniqueness of Jesus in bringing salvation.

In the West today, freedom of religion means we do not face the pressure to bow to a single power. But there is a more subtle coercion – believing and declaring that any one truth claim is truer than the rest is highly unpopular. We live in a culture where truth is individualised and relative. Terms like 'post-truth' and 'fake news' have become part of our everyday language in recent times. The whole area of what truth is, and whether it is even possible to have absolute truth, seems to be very much under attack. We can appear to promise to tell 'my truth, my own truth and nothing but my truth.' This is not to play down the importance of personal lived experience but to say that there are still some things that are utterly true, whatever our own experience may be. In the midst of this cultural pressure, we must be strong enough to hold onto the utter exclusivity and authority of Jesus and continue to be brave in standing firm. Our friend, the theologian and fellow Youth for Christ alumnus, Ajith Fernando, puts it this way:

11 F. Skinner, *Frank Skinner* (London: Arrow Books, 2001), p. 96.

Pluralists say there is no such thing as absolute truth. We cannot say that. For the Creator of the world has given humanity a unique and once-for-all message in the person and work of the Lord of the universe: Jesus Christ.[12]

We have more religious liberty in the UK than almost any other nation on earth. We need to know our actual freedoms to share the gospel, before moaning about those freedoms we perceive that we are losing. Throughout our history, freedom of religion and belief has always been a significant issue and this remains the case for our members today. We may not face the threat of death like many of our spiritual brothers, sisters, fathers and mothers, but we must resolve to stand firm against the temptation to drop the exclusive claim of Jesus that he is *the* way, *the* truth and *the* life. Not all roads lead to God.

The exclusivity of Jesus has been, is now and always will be an unpopular and contested claim. However, that must not stop us from standing for the truth of this in every age. But for each generation, winds of cultural change and public opinion can create a landscape against which it can be tempting to question biblical values on specific issues in that day. Perhaps the example of this in our times is with regard to same-sex marriage. In a matter of decades, attitudes have completely changed.

In 1975, just 16% of people thought that homosexual couples should be allowed to marry each other. In 2014, this had more than quadrupled to 69%.[13] The writer Douglas Murray describes how a change of view can even take place in the mind of a senior politician – not in decades, but in a matter of years. In May 2013, the MP Nicky Morgan voted against the law introducing gay marriage. A year later, she said that she supported gay marriage and would

---

12 A. Fernando, *Sharing the Truth in Love: How to relate to people of other faiths* (Grand Rapids: Discovery House Publishing, 2001), p. 185.

13 Ipsos, 'Dramatic Change in Attitudes towards Gay Couples', 23 April 2014, https://www.ipsos.com/en-uk/dramatic-change-attitudes-towards-gay-couples (accessed 23 October 2024).

vote for it had it not already become law. Just one year after that, she was declaring that the views that she herself had held two years earlier were not just 'extreme' but 'fundamentally un-British'.[14]

For us evangelicals, we believe that marriage is a God-given gift, between a man and a woman and that the Bible affirms this in creation, in Jesus' teaching and Paul's writings.[15] To believe this and verbalise it in 1975 would have been uncontroversial, but to do so today in some contexts risks being branded homophobic and hateful and being cancelled. The politician Tim Farron found this to be the case in June 2017. Farron resigned as leader of the Liberal Democrats after repeated questioning about his biblically faithful views on marriage. In his departing speech he said, 'To be a political leader – especially of a progressive liberal party – and to live as a committed Christian, to hold faithfully to the Bible's teaching, has felt impossible for me.'[16] And this is the cost he has felt: 'The loss that I have experienced since then was the loss of reputation, standing and even dignity.'

Most of us don't find ourselves in high public office, but it can require similar levels of bravery to stand firm, hold to the good news and speak up in our social circles, workplaces and communities. And this is not the only issue on which we may be at odds with mainstream views, or at least those that appear to be holding sway most loudly or with the biggest platforms. From issues of racial justice, to how we treat the marginalised; from abortion to euthanasia; from how we spend our money to what we watch on our screens – and on many more issues – we need to tune our ears to the voice of the Shepherd and not be swept along with the rest of the sheep. This was shown in November 2024 with

---

14 D. Murray, *The Madness of Crowds: Gender, race and agenda* (London: Bloomsbury, 2019), pp. 18–19.

15 Genesis 2:24, Matthew 19:5, Ephesians 5:31.

16 T. Farron, *A Better Ambition: Confessions of a faithful Liberal* (London: SPCK, 2019), p. 288.

the private members' bill on assisted dying being brought to the House of Commons for a second reading. Though, tragically, the vote at this stage went in favour of allowing people to end their lives prematurely,[17] we were able to sound a different tune. We galvanised over 1,200 Christian leaders to sign a shared letter,[18] stood with leaders of other faith groups in another shared letter that got wide secular media coverage[19] and helped thousands of our members to act individually too in prayer and writing to their local MP. The parliamentary vote was very close and we were able to help catalyse the Church to tell a different story to the secular culture. At the time of writing, we don't know whether this proposal will pass into law, but we can guarantee that the Evangelical Alliance will continue to do all we can to stand up for the sanctity of life and the need to show compassion in sharing in the suffering of those around us as opposed to enabling them to end it through assisted suicide.

In the political arena, one of the important roles we play as the Evangelical Alliance is taking a brave stance for all of us. We have an advocacy team serving across all four nations of the UK, regularly meeting and speaking up in Westminster, Holyrood, the Senedd and Stormont. Gavin also does a fair amount of advocacy work within his role, meeting and engaging across the UK on behalf of the Evangelical Church. One of our favourite examples of this work and its effectiveness is to do with a proposal around what are known as 'out-of-school settings'. There was a proposal to change the law in the last decade that, if passed, would have enabled

17 H. Zeffman and K. Whannel, 'Tears, Hope and Fear as Assisted Dying Bill Passed', BBC News, 30 November 2024, https://www.bbc.co.uk/news/articles/crmzgmz1meno (accessed 19 December 2024).

18 D. Webster, 'More Than 1200 Christian Leaders Join Letter to MPs Opposing Assisted Dying Plans', Evangelical Alliance, 21 November 2024, https://www.eauk.org/news-and-views/hundreds-of-christian-leaders-are-speaking-out-against-assisted-dying-plans-will-you-join-them (accessed 19 December 2024).

19 J. Eastham, 'Britain's Religious Leaders Unite against Assisted Dying in Major Intervention', 24 November 2024, The Telegraph, https://www.telegraph.co.uk/politics/2024/11/24/assisted-dying-bill-religious-leaders-letter-duty-to-die/ (accessed 19 December 2024).

government groups to register, regulate and inspect Sunday schools and youth groups in our churches and essentially critique and assess what was being said and taught. Public regulation of private religion? Such a restriction on religious freedom being proposed in the UK sounded more like something you might find in North Korea. So, we as the Evangelical Alliance spoke up on behalf of the Church and, as a result, the bill was shelved – at least for now.

We want to encourage leaders to be brave in standing firm. As leaders of the Church, we can be as vulnerable to conforming to culture as anyone else. At the time of writing, there is painful and hostile disagreement in some of the major denominations on the issue of marriage. For all of us, it would be easier, more palatable and popular to fall in line with the majority view, but submitting to the authority of God and Scripture means we have to be brave.

And as we take the brave step of keeping the Bible as our primary basis for belief in all things, there are two further things to consider. First, we need constant wisdom for when we speak up and the tone with which we do it. Second, we need to remember we are good news people. When we are under pressure to conform, we can take opportunities to get on the front foot and speak positively about the hope that we have. Tim Farron is an admirable example of this. In what could have been a resignation speech full of self-pity and bitterness, he sought to point to Jesus.

> I thoroughly love my party. Imagine how proud I am to lead this party. And then imagine what would lead me to voluntarily relinquish that honour. In the words of Isaac Watts, it would have to be something 'so amazing, so divine, [it] demands my heart, my life, my all'.[20]

---

20 J. Elgot, 'Tim Farron Resigns: Fresh-faced Lib Dem hampered by his faith', 14 June 2017, *The Guardian*, https://www.theguardian.com/politics/2017/jun/14/tim-farron-resigns-liberal-democrats-fresh-face-struggled-with-questions-over-his-christianity (accessed 23 October 2024).

Kind in standing firm

To be kind in standing firm, we have to follow the biblical mandate for our own lives, while also seeing others as people made in the image of God. Jesus commands us to love one another, as he loves us. We in turn need to demonstrate God's love in our actions, thoughts and words towards one another. Jesus is 'full of grace and truth' (John 1:14). He embodies the posture he commands. Following him means that even if someone does something that upsets or offends us, we still have to demonstrate this love and not choose to place judgement on others where we shouldn't. As we seek to serve people, we must not compromise on truth. But, at the same time, we must treat people with the dignity, integrity and love that they deserve.

One of our aims is to be the type of evangelicals that people encounter and they can't say that we're unkind. We have no problem with someone disagreeing with the substance of what we stand for – but please never let it be said that we don't embody the kindness of Jesus. We often find on social media that people will say things like 'All evangelicals are horrible and want nothing to do with people like me.' When we spot this happening, we will go out of our way to offer someone an opportunity to meet up to chat and to move beyond lazy stereotypes. Let's show people in a humanised form what it means to be good news people in a bad news world. We are wholeheartedly committed to being loving and kind while remaining brave. One of the challenges is society says that we must not question anything, challenge anything or speak truth that might offend in any way. In reality, one of the most unkind things we can do is to never speak the truth to those we love. We want to be kind, we want to stand firm and we will fight not to lose friends because we disagree with them. Equally, we are desperate for our friends to encounter Jesus – so in the midst of this, we are tolerant and loving but we are also pointing people towards the Jesus we live for.

As we've said, the Evangelical Alliance's advocacy team often speaks out on free speech and religious liberties. These issues are perhaps characterised as areas of public policy that are more brave than kind, more truth than grace. But we also celebrate the advocacy we have done that is driven by a compassionate and kind heart for the last and the least. The pioneering work of Home for Good that inspired the Church to explore fostering and adoption, also recognised that there were some solutions in that field that would require systemic change and would need political engagement alongside church mobilisation. Proverbs 31:8 exhorts us to speak up for those who cannot speak up for themselves. This sort of advocacy is as kind as it is brave.

And on the issue of same-sex marriage, our bravery must be surpassed by our kindness. Where members of the LGBTQ+ community are mistreated, we must call it out and stand with them. This too can require great bravery in some contexts. And where the Church has been unkind and unwelcoming in the past we must repent and make sure that our communities demonstrate the radical generosity and grace of Jesus. We must remind ourselves that kindness does not equal approval. After all, the abundant kindness of Jesus in laying down his life for us was in order to liberate us from our sin and brokenness, not as an endorsement of it. We can be profoundly kind without this being taken as a sign that we affirm the choices and lifestyles people are pursuing.

Brave in reaching out

There are few better blueprints for gospel proclamation and church growth than the opening chapters of Acts.[21] Jesus is taken up to heaven, the Holy Spirit fills the disciples, the global launch party of the Church is inaugurated with Peter preaching to the crowd,

---

21 For a more thorough exposition of these themes, check out Calver and Calver, *Unleashed*, p. 32.

a beggar is healed, the authorities arrest Peter and John, and then they are released. It is an explosion of activity and increase. What happens next is particularly insightful. The natural inclination of many leaders at this point, probably including ourselves, would be to form a three-year strategic plan for the next stage of the mission. But what the embryonic Church does is pray.

At this vital stage of development of the world's most successful start-up, the leaders stop. And pray.

Throughout this book, we hope you are hearing from us an incessant and hopeful desire to see the gospel of Jesus Christ impact every corner of the UK and beyond. Many of these pages are about the passion and practices we believe we're being called to adopt if we're to see this happen. But we want to be crystal clear that we believe that what underpins it all is a deep commitment to prayer. We know it is 'Not by power nor by power, but by [his] Spirit' (Zechariah 4:6). And when it comes to being gospel people, prayer is the bedrock. But what the early church prayed for is even more instructive.

In Acts 4:23–31, we get a seat at one of the fiery prayer meetings of the Acts church at a pivotal moment. Under intense scrutiny and attack from the authorities, many of us would pray for a change in circumstances. Seeing 3,000 new believers, many of us would pray for results. But what they pray for is to be bold: 'Now Lord, consider their threats and enable your servants to speak your word with great boldness' (Acts 4:29).

What might it look like if the content of our twenty-first-century prayer meetings, church services and home groups looked more like that of the early church. Perhaps one of the reasons we aren't seeing the expansive growth we see in the book of Acts is that we aren't praying Acts-like prayers. Let's make boldness our prayer.

You would be forgiven for thinking when you meet one of us, that we never struggle when it comes to putting ourselves out there to share Jesus. But evangelists are notoriously misunderstood when it comes to the amount of courage they have. Almost all of us care what people think of us and those who share the gospel are not immune. When we speak at events and in churches and give people the opportunity to respond, there is a vulnerable moment when we fear no one will come forward or put their hand in the air, even though we know that the results are the work of the Holy Spirit. It can be even more daunting when speaking one-on-one to friends, neighbours or strangers. We have both had countless moments of 'bottling it' as well as occasions when we have put ourselves out there.

I, Phil, experienced this agony recently where I felt God nudge me at the beginning of the Easter holidays to buy Easter eggs for the families on our street, to deliver them as a family door-to-door. We also decided to offer to pray for our neighbours as we delivered the eggs and, where appropriate, to share the gospel. In my weakness, tiredness and humanity, there was as much dread as there was excitement. Reluctance dominated my thoughts in the week before. But I asked a friend to hold me accountable and on Good Friday, the Knoxes knocked on doors with chocolate blessings and offers of intercession.

As I reflected on the experience, I was reminded of this quote from the evangelist Robin Gamble which sums up the tension we face:

> Despite what everyone seems to think, evangelists are not the ones who find it easy, they do not have an endless supply of inner boldness; they are simply the ones that do it, and the more they do it, the better at it they become.[22]

But the act of obedience also reminded me how open people are in this season. There were some homes that took the egg and were hesitant in accepting prayer, but they were grateful nonetheless.

---

22 R. Gamble, *Jesus the Evangelist: Doing it his way in my world* (Eastbourne: David C. Cook, 2009), p. 229.

But there were others who were remarkably open. One woman described herself as a 'new pagan' but said she had really struggled since moving to the area. After we prayed, her eyes were filled with tears. Another neighbour spoke of his bereavement, having recently lost his dad to cancer.

However, the most encouraging encounter came when two late-teenagers answered the door. They accepted the offer of prayer enthusiastically and were then joined by their mum. She shared how she had been recently exploring 'spiritual stuff'. She had tried Islam, Buddhism and was still searching. My wife Dani and I listened to her story and then offered to share ours. By the end of the conversation, she said she would love to talk further and the teenage son confessed that he had been studying the Bible with his friend and they would both like to come to our church. The unnecessary anxiety, the cost of the eggs and the summoning up of the courage to knock on that first door were more than worth it for that one moment of encouragement.

Incidentally, the other reflection was the isolation that is the lived experience of so many people. One couple answered the door and explained their surprise because no one ever visited them or rang the doorbell. We live amidst an epidemic of loneliness, where so many people have never been more disconnected to their community.

We perhaps all need to be a little braver and reach out to others. Like Phil, I, Gavin, was recently involved in some street outreach in my local community. Others from the church seemed to expect me to be the expert at starting conversations and praying for people on our local high street. The fear and dread kicked in but, like for the Knoxes, this was not to be the end of the story. I stood nervously outside the local tube station and started up a conversation with a young man who seemed overwhelmed. He had a bad leg injury and after some conversation was happy for me to pray for his leg. I'd love to say that there was an instant miraculous healing, but there wasn't. However, there was an overwhelming sense of peace as I prayed and the young man said that he had felt comforted and helped before heading off to jump on a bus. I will never know what he said about this moment to others he met later that day but I do know that something of the kingdom was shared between us. Too often we can keep this in our church buildings but we need to brave enough to overflow into our communities. Because I stepped up, I had the joy of praying for others in my community. We must fight the fear and the people-pleasing and step up to be brave.

Kind in reaching out

Our spiritual fathers and mothers in the early church were not just brave. Their bold prayers, words and activities were propagated in a culture of kindness. The opening chapters of Acts are punctuated with rhythms of compassion. They 'sold property and possessions to give to anyone who had need' (Acts 2:45) and within their community they share all they have (Acts 4:32). Peter and John have no money with them when they encounter a lame man outside the Temple, so give what they have and he is healed (Acts 3:1–10).

What is striking, when you read all these verses, is that right next to each of them is reference to gospel communication. It seems that faith-sharing in word and deed were inseparable for the apostles. Kindness and bravery go hand in hand.

This balance is at the heart of one of the profound challenges facing the Church today. Most of us tend to lean towards either kind deeds *or* brave words – one at the expense of the other. Many churches and organisations have exceptional programmes that demonstrate God's love to people in a practical way, but rarely step out to talk about him. Others courageously shout loudly from street corners but lack the winsomeness or gentleness that might earn them a more favourable hearing.

In Acts 6, we read of the power and fruit of bold preaching and compassionate care. The twelve apostles enlarge their team to ensure that their first-century foodbanks stay open and that widows are looked after. As a result, not only does this work continue, but the apostles are released to pray and preach the gospel. The fruit of this marriage of bravery and kindness is not a coincidence: 'So the word of God spread. The number of disciples in Jerusalem increased rapidly, and a large number of priests became obedient to the faith' (Acts 6:7).

This theme of *how* we talk about Jesus continues throughout the New Testament. Some of our favourite passages about sharing the gospel give clear instruction around the tone of communication as much as the content. Paul, writing to the church in Colossae asks them to pray for him, that doors would open for his message and that he would have clarity in his proclamation (Colossians 4:3–5). But this is followed up in the following verse with these words: 'Let your conversation be always full of grace' (verse 6). In a world where the arena of opposing views are angry panel discussions and exchanges on social media written entirely in caps lock, our gospel interactions are to be open-palmed, smile-drenched and grace-filled.

Peter follows suit in his letter to those scattered across the provinces. In an oft-quoted verse of those whose passion is apologetics, he encourages us to 'Always be prepared to give an answer to anyone who asks you to give the reason for the hope that you have' (1 Peter 3:15). This mandate is vital. How many opportunities do we individually and corporately fail to make the most of because we are underprepared to share our story of what God has done for us? But, like his New Testament brother Paul, Peter is quick to follow up with a note on how we share, 'But do this with gentleness and respect'. It is possible to 'win' a factual argument with an unbeliever but do so in such a way that it pushes them further away. It is also possible to 'lose' an argument but do so with such kindness that they end up trusting Jesus, or at least want to find out more.

And when reaching out, we discover that it is the kindness of God that so many people respond to. The *Finding Jesus* research asked almost 300 people who had become Christians as adults in the last five years about their journeys to faith. When participants were asked which aspect of the gospel most drew them to Jesus, the most compelling attraction was 'That Jesus loves me.'[23]

Brave and kind in relationship

These two godly traits also complement each other when we are in relationship with one another. First, there can be situations where someone is struggling and needs great kindness. In such moments, we can often hesitate. We ask ourselves things like, 'Do they really need our help?', 'What if they become dependent on me?', 'Will they think I'm being kind with an agenda?' To take the kind step often means overcoming our fears about what it will cost us and what others will think. It is a brave step.

And second, kindness can sometimes mean challenging others because we love them. It sometimes seems that the world has tried to steal the word 'kindness' and make it mean not disagreeing, or not questioning anything, or an absolute acceptance and endorsement of everything without any need to ever change. This simply is not kind at all. Kindness instead is treating everyone as someone made in the image of God and with all the dignity and love that this requires. Love sometimes means change for all of us. The American author and minister Max Lucado says that 'God loves you just the way you are, but He refuses to leave you there. He wants you to be just like Jesus.'[24] Kindness loves others but also longs for all of us

---

23 *Finding Jesus* (2025), www.findingjesus.co.uk

24 M. Lucado, 'Just Like Jesus', https://maxlucado.com/products/just-like-jesus/ (accessed 20 November 2024).

to be more like Jesus. A compassionate challenge from a friend is sometimes the kindest thing possible. As it says in Proverbs 27:6 'Wounds from a friend can be trusted'. We need to be profoundly kind, in the purest form of its meaning.

Brave and kind *together*

The reason this is the first of the postures we are exploring in this book is because it is the one I, Gavin, sensed the Lord told me to lean into in this season. When I was spending time prayerfully considering whether or not to apply for the role of CEO of the Evangelical Alliance back in 2019, the Lord was very clear with me that this was how we needed to stand as good news people in the years ahead. First, it was very clear to me that we needed to be braver in the days ahead than we have ever been before. We need to be brave and resilient, building up the Church, sticking to the truth, taking bullets for local churches so they don't always have to. We need to be prepared to be brave – and no one is born brave. For us, one of the bravest people in Scripture is Esther. When she goes to visit the king, she risks the most radical of haircuts just for turning up – she could have had her head chopped off simply for being in his presence. But she chooses to be brave nonetheless. In our day, we need to be brave – outrageously brave – and go for it.

It is easier to be brave when you are with others. People rarely act boldly in isolation. When we unite and stick together, we inspire bravery in one another. We hope that this is what we can contribute as the Evangelical Alliance, as we play our part in helping to strengthen the Evangelical Church at this challenging time. We are here for you. We have an opportunity to extend our prophetic imaginations as to what is possible, and be clear on what we believe, without missing the chance to share our message with others. In other words, we are all being given an opportunity to be braver together.

And unity with other good news Christians should also make us kinder. Seeing others reach out with love should inspire that same compassion in us. Like the Acts church responding to the needs around them, we can winsomely and graciously join in with the team game of bringing light into the darkness and meeting human, social and spiritual needs. And being kind also means gentle correction where brothers and sisters tend towards being unkind in their boldness and determination to be right. For all these reasons we need to hold this posture – but we do so as one.

Taking it further

- Take a moment to reflect on where in your life you need to be braver. Where might the Lord be calling you to stand firm? Then ask the Holy Spirit to reveal where your heart, words and actions need to be kinder. Consider what proactive steps you could take to put these values into action. Write them down and ask someone you trust to hold you accountable to them.
- In your personal prayer life, when you consider what and who you pray for, might you remember the Acts 4 prayer meeting and spend some time asking the Lord for boldness each day to live and speak in a way that encourages others to follow Jesus.
- Could you consider a small initiative on your road like Phil and his family undertook with the Easter eggs? Could you find an occasion to give a gift and offer to pray? You may find people are far more open than you would think.

Recommended reading

Beautiful Resistance: The joy of conviction in a culture of compromise by Jon Tyson (New York: Random House, 2020) – A bold invitation to the kind of discipleship needed to resist embracing our culture and to remain distinct from it, replacing compromise with conviction.

Speak Up: A brief guide to the law and your gospel freedoms (Evangelical Alliance and Lawyers' Christian Fellowship, 2022) – *Speak Up* is designed to equip and inspire Christians with confidence and knowledge of the current legal freedoms we have to share our faith. It is a simple guide to your rights and responsibilities when sharing your faith in the workplace and community. Get a copy of it here: https://www.eauk.org/what-we-do/initiatives/speak-up

Unleashed: The Acts church today by Gavin and Anne Calver (London: IVP, 2020) – What might it look like to live like the Acts church today? Working through the first half of the book of Acts, this engaging and practical book challenges us to consider how we might need to return to the oldest way of doing church and reach our communities through words, works and wonders.

The themes of this chapter can be explored further using small group resources, videos and discussion questions. Delve deeper at www.goodnewspeople.church

5

We need to be culturally relevant without selling out

We don't have to make the Bible relevant – it is – but we have
to show its relevance.
Rick Warren[1]

Our next posture describes how we relate to the rapidly changing
culture around us. If it feels to you like the world is speeding up, you
are not alone. The world we live in now would be unrecognisable
to those who lived in the same postcode as us 100 years ago. When
we make comparisons like this, we can instinctively think about
technology and the dramatic shifts that the digital revolution
has brought to the way we work, interact and relax. But also
consider the sweeping developments in terms of architecture,
fashion, media, travel, population, entertainment and societal
worldviews. The pace of change has been dizzying. For some it
has been exhilarating, for others disorientating, but for all of us
it has been unavoidable.

Over the next decade, we see no let-up in the speed of cultural
shift. That is why this posture matters as we decide as good news
people how we will respond to the swirling winds of constant
change. Will we set our face resolutely against the hurricane and
keep doing what we have always done? Or will we allow the breeze
to blow us wherever it pleases? Our plea to the Church in these

---

1 M. Duduit, 'Purpose-driven Preaching: An interview with Rick Warren', Preaching.
com, https://www.preaching.com/articles/purpose-driven-preaching-an-interview-
with-rick-warren/ (accessed 20 November 2024).

times is that the substance needs to stay the same but the methods should always adapt to the times. Or, as American Founding Father Thomas Jefferson more eloquently expressed it, 'In matters of style, swim with the current; in matters of principle, stand like a rock.'[2]

This, perhaps more than the other postures, is a 'look forward' chapter. We want to enthuse you with what the Church could look like and invite you to play your part.

Blockbuster decisions

Many years ago, I, Gavin, was in my local Blockbuster video shop – when such places still existed. Anne and I had not yet started a family and I found myself noticing this dad with two young children trying to pick out a film to watch. I felt like the Lord pointed something out to me… What if the kids desperately wanted to watch *Dumbo* but the dad really wants to watch *Rambo*? Which video cassette (as was the format back then) would they take home to enjoy together as a family? Even as I write this, it feels a bit ridiculous because, let's be honest, it is clearly going to be *Dumbo*. Irrespective of the preferences of the more mature, if everyone is going to access the film and if its content is going to be appropriate for the less mature, you would have to make that right decision and watch the family-friendly film about a flying elephant.

A few years later, I had young children too and I faced a similar dilemma. My parents, who live in the USA, came to stay. Before we had our kids, my parents would come and we would watch an episode of *Poirot* and have a curry together. However, after kids came along, the curry was replaced with hamburgers and chips and *Poirot* with *Peppa Pig*. It struck me that in families we always

---

2 T. Rhoades, 'In Matters of Style, Swim with the Current. In Matters of Principle, Stand Like a Rock', Chemistry Staffing, https://blog.chemistrystaffing.com/in-matters-of-style-swim-with-the-current.-in-matters-of-principle-stand-like-a-rock (accessed 20 November 2024).

accommodate the least mature in order to make them feel part of something, included and involved.

This is such an important lesson for us as a Church. We cannot expect those who are less mature in the faith, or indeed have no faith, to meet us exactly where we are and just fit in. The more spiritually mature must be willing to sacrifice their own preferences and not just expect the less experienced to do so – but our default has become to connect with the more spiritually mature. In a church context, when it comes to outreach and evangelism, this is not so much an age thing as an issue of spiritual maturity and depth of understanding. We long for us to be culturally relevant and accessible to those who do not yet know Jesus, while standing firm on what we believe without compromise. It is so simple, and possible, to be culturally relevant without selling out on our content.

When James Hudson-Taylor went to China and founded the China Inland Mission (now OMF International), he wore the local dress, learnt the language, ate local food and more – all so that he could create a platform for the gospel.[3] People like him are celebrated as missionary heroes for all they did to contextualise the gospel message in foreign lands. However, we so often fail to do similar things in our own communities in order to contextualise the unchanging message within our own space and make Jesus known.

For us both, the *substance* of all we believe and hold to is unchangeable but the *style* should be able to change like the wind. We both have a background in youth ministry and so we are very used to reimagining style in order to engage with new generations. We both joined Youth for Christ when the internet was still quite new, social media did not exist and mobile phones were used for making phone calls and nothing more. Over our time serving at Youth for Christ, all these things became vital components of

3 OMF International, https://omf.org/about-us/our-story/ (accessed 23 October 2024).

culture – and there were so many other changes along the way too. These rapid changes meant that you were continually altering the style of work with young people, while retaining the substance of the message that never changes.

A stormy cultural forecast

High winds are rarely fun when you are exposed to them. It can be even worse when you are in a tent. I, Phil, remember an unfortunate camping experience in which the family tent was set up in fair weather. But before long, a gentle breeze had turned to full-blown typhoon-like gusts and the patter of raindrops to a deluge. In religious language, it was a squall of 'biblical' proportions. The cheap canvas was ill-equipped to cope with the conditions. I recall the longing for a break from the relentless gale and being eager for the calm of morning. By the time dawn broke, the children's air beds were floating on the puddles. The car was a welcome shelter. The tent went in the bin.

In Chapter 4, we identified a decreasing tolerance for biblically faithful views and a temptation to water down what we believe to make it more palatable to the world. Over the coming years, we see no change in the cultural weather forecast as society continues to worship at the altar of tolerance and individualism. The allure of adjusting our theology to suit the times is nothing new. In his own era of competing worldviews, Paul offers us a biblical framework for stylistically swimming with the current and ideologically standing on the rock.

When Paul writes to the Christians in Ephesus about the substance or content of what they believe, he describes maturity as not being 'tossed back and forth by the waves, and blown here and there by every wind of doctrine' (Ephesians 4:14). It is comforting to think that the early church communities felt similar pressures to us to bend their beliefs in line with the world around them. They too had to be warned against conforming. As we sail through the choppy waters of our times, as trusting God and the Bible becomes increasingly unpopular, we can take heart from these verses. In nautical terms, we need to hold our course as well as our nerve. But Paul also reminds us of our brave and kind posture in the very next verse: 'Instead, speaking the truth in love, we will grow up to become in every respect the mature body of him who is the head, that is, Christ' (Ephesians 4:15).

And in another letter, this time to his protégé Timothy, Paul expresses his concern that we can so easily opt to change what God says to suit our own needs and wants: 'Instead, to suit their own desires, they will gather round them a great number of teachers to say what their itching ears want to hear' (2 Timothy 4:3). The Bible's encouragement is to hold firm to the essence of the gospel and the teachings of the Bible, no matter how strong or subtle the temptation to ditch or adapt them.

A masterclass in methodology

We have talked about substance. Now we turn to style – and we see Paul rewriting the rulebook of cultural engagement. When he is in Athens, he is distressed to see the extent of idol worship in the city. He earns a hearing at the Areopagus, an Athenian rocky outcrop which was the setting for the debates of local philosophers and leaders. Observe with us what he does next:

Paul then stood up in the meeting of the Areopagus and said: 'People of Athens! I see that in every way you are very religious. For as I walked around and looked carefully at your objects of worship, I even found an altar with this inscription: TO AN UNKNOWN GOD. So you are ignorant of the very thing you worship – and this is what I am going to proclaim to you.

'The God who made the world and everything in it is the Lord of heaven and earth and does not live in temples built by human hands. And he is not served by human hands, as if he needed anything. Rather, he himself gives everyone life and breath and everything else. From one man he made all the nations, that they should inhabit the whole earth; and he marked out their appointed times in history and the boundaries of their lands. God did this so that they would seek him and perhaps reach out for him and find him, though he is not far from any one of us. "For in him we live and move and have our being." As some of your own poets have said, "We are his offspring."'
(Acts 17:22–28)

'I see that in every way you are very religious.' Paul finds common humanity and identifies with them. He too is very religious. Whether it is a mutual interest in football, hipster coffee, gardening, salsa, Taylor Swift, 1980s' cartoons or 1990s' vinyl, we build chemistry with people by finding similar passions. The best gospel connections take place on common ground.

'I walked around and looked carefully at your objects of worship.' He looks at the cultural markers of their day. You get the impression from this that Paul enjoyed people watching. In a coffee shop, he would be the one in the chair facing the rest of the room. But this was not because he was nosy, it was because he was intentionally looking for ways to connect the story of God to the contextual story wherever he found himself.

'TO AN UNKNOWN GOD.' Here we see Paul's genius. In the polytheistic marketplace, he spots an altar to the unknowable, an ode to no one, an absent phantom deity, a road to nowhere. And he builds a bridge. He basically says, 'Guys, you know that god that you don't know? Well, I know who he is. Let me tell you about him.'

'The God who made the world and everything in it is the Lord of heaven and earth.' Having built his bridge of cultural connection he now drives the good news across it into the hearts of his listeners. Note that the essence of the message is still the heart of the good news. He still talks about Jesus and his victory over the grave (verse 31). He still calls people to repent and believe (verse 30).

Make the beautiful news make sense

In the spring of 2016, a new bridge in Copenhagen was meant to be opened to the public for the first time. The Inderhavnsbroen was designed to connect the seventeenth-century waterfront to the islands across the city's harbour. Its design was as clever as its nickname was romantic. 'The Kissing Bridge' was so christened because each side had a retractable arm that opened and closed to allow ships to pass through. When they 'kissed' in the middle, the alignment meant people could cross. Except they didn't quite kiss. The small matter of six to eight centimetres of misalignment meant an expensive delay.

Throughout the centuries of the Church, generations of missionaries, evangelists, pastors, friends, co-workers, neighbours and preachers have been inspired to build bridges that 'kiss' and make the beautiful news make sense. Paul's masterclass on Mars Hill in Athens is a wonderful example and mandate of how we are to do that, and communicate the unchanging gospel to an everchanging world. On that first-century day at the Areopagus, some were reached by Paul's creativity and God's grace (verse 34). In the millennia since, billions more have followed.

We recognise this section may apply more to those who influence style, especially those with leadership responsibilities in their churches. But it is helpful for all of us to adopt this posture and look forward with creativity and hope to the future of the Church. The rapidly changing times must provoke us as good news people to consider how our gatherings and practices engage with the world in a culturally relevant way. The tension we hold is that we must do so without selling out or losing the gritty, distinctive essence of the substance.

In this next section, we will explore the principles behind effective cultural engagement and celebrate the people who are doing this well. We hope you are inspired through these to think about how it might look in your context, whatever the size, shape or tribe of your church.

EPIC engagement

So what might this look like in practice for each of us?

A while ago, at a Youth for Christ staff conference, the theologian Leonard Sweet said something about this that has continued to shape our thinking. He said that anything that works in engaging today's society and culture is EPIC:

Experiential
Participative
Image-driven
Connected[4]

Stylistically, if we are going to connect with today's culture then perhaps we too have to become more EPIC. What does this mean for us in respect of style? We think a great example of something EPIC in in our culture is IKEA.

I, Gavin, remember only too well the IKEA shop opening in Croydon near where I grew up in south-east London. Back then, this new type of shop was amazing – especially when compared

---

4 Leonard has written in detail about this in his book, *Postmodern Pilgrims: A 1st century passion for a 21st century church* (Nashville: Broadman and Holman Publishers, 2000) and in numerous articles that can be found on Leonard Sweet, https://leonardsweet.com (accessed 23 October 2024).

with any other furniture place. As a young man, I could not imagine many things that were more boring than going furniture shopping – but IKEA changed the game altogether. It was so experiential. In place of the usual shop floor was a path that led you on a journey, all around the shop. You weren't simply looking for a product as quickly as possible – it was more like embarking on an experience. You didn't feel like you were on a boring shopping trip, you were on a journey.

It was also participatory. You actively got involved and you tried stuff. If you wanted to buy a sofa then you sat on lots of different ones. You could see how the springs worked. You could use a computer screen to see what colour of sofa would best suit the decor of your lounge. You were not an objective bystander who might purchase from the outside, you were involved in the whole process. The entire time was participatory not passive.

IKEA is also image-driven – from its logo to the setup of the rooms, from its distinctive brand colours to the style of furniture. When you go to someone's house for dinner, or you turn up at a church, you can immediately spot the IKEA furniture. There is a distinctive look and feel to it, it's image-driven.

Finally, IKEA is connected. Before IKEA came along, you would go to a kitchen warehouse to buy a kitchen. But IKEA did it so differently. You didn't just buy a kitchen – you looked at a number of mocked up kitchens. These were not simply warehouse models. They had trinkets and pictures, a clock on the wall, pots and pans, glasses, knives and forks, plates. You could walk around it. This was not a kitchen to buy off-the-shelf but one that you could imagine being in your house. Instead of thinking 'they're alright kitchen cabinets' you thought 'that could be my kitchen'.

And being EPIC is not restricted to IKEA. Think of other culturally successful brands such as Starbucks, Parkrun, Fortnite or Apple and the EPIC principles continue to apply as strongly. They are all Experiential, Participative, Image-driven and Connected. We are both convinced that it is equally possible to have a style of church that appeals to today's culture just as creatively without having to compromise on any of the substance. All over the world, every day of the week, different Christians are contextualising the style in order to share the substance of the message of Jesus with those around them. Perhaps here in the UK, the time has come for us to ask where we need to make EPIC changes to our style to reach people locally here too without any compromise over the substance. There is no 'one size fits all' and we hope the principles and examples that we will use will help you think creatively about how you can adapt to be even more fruitful where you are.

Make yourself at home

We have spoken about the great joy of seeing a different church in action every week and interacting with leaders almost every day. One of the great blessings of this is that we get to see the ways in which the UK Church is culturally adapting. Many churches are successfully building twenty-first-century bridges across which the good news is spreading. They are creating innovative church environments that embody the gospel but connect with both believers and not-yet believers where they are at. We want to share some of these innovations with you to help us all as we seek to connect with today's generations.

We see features and facets of EPIC in almost every church setting. But in a world that is not showing any signs of standing still, neither can we. We must keep asking ourselves how we should reimagine and re-embody our gatherings, messages, routines, rhythms and relationships. We hope that some of the stories and ideas that follow give you inspiration and encouragement for your context.

Our framework as we explore some great practice in this area is a family home. The imagery of home has powerful resonance for people today for a few reasons. One of the most dominant worldviews in our culture today is what is known as 'expressive individualism'. It is the narrative we are bombarded with that urges us to trust our feelings and be our authentic selves.[5] Despite its relentless reinforcement, many people long for community. The Church is the truest expression of family in its rightful place, under God's rule.

As the cultural stories of progress and consumerism crumble in people's minds and we work out how to live in the 'permacrisis', many have a growing sense of lostness. To those who are lost, the call of the gospel is 'Come home.' And when we, like the prodigal in the parable, come to our senses and stumble back to the Father, the words we hear are 'Welcome home.'

We are far less likely to live in the place where we were born or grew up than previous generations. While there are many benefits to modern mobility, uprootedness can mean we no longer feel we have a place to call home. A decade-long study of 7,100 Americans sought to discern how moving affects people. Soberingly, it found that moving is associated with lower levels of wellbeing, higher stress levels and fewer positive social relationships, especially in younger people.[6] Interior design has become a quasi-religion. Fuelled by DIY and furniture businesses (including the aforementioned Swedish meatball-serving one), we are spending more and more on making our houses into homes.

All these factors make home a compelling contemporary theme. We are not surprised when we visit growing churches and they have large, lit displays or messaging on the homepage of their website declaring 'Welcome home.' So, we are going to take you on a tour of an imaginary home, and as we do so, each room will correspond

---

5 For a comprehensive definition and explanation, our friends Jo Frost and Peter Lynas unpack this worldview in *Being Human: A new lens for our cultural conversations* (London: Hodder & Stoughton, 2023).

6 D. Grothe, *The Power of Place: Choosing stability in a rootless age* (Nashville: Nelson Books, 2021), p. 25.

to a different area of church life that we think needs some Spirit-inspired innovation and bridgebuilding cultural connection in the years ahead.

The hallway

When you walk into someone's house, you immediately get a feel for what the family who live there are like. The photos on the walls may tell something of their story, whether you receive a handshake or a hug will tell you something of the formality of the situation, whether they are 'shoes off' or 'shoes on' may tell you how new their carpets are! A warm welcome changes everything. We know the feeling of arriving at a friend's house to be embraced, greeted with a cup of coffee, sinking into the sofa ready for laughter and honest conversation. It feels like home from home.

What is our experience of welcome like at church? We have observed that growing churches have a world-class welcome. When cars are advertised, the manufacturer measures and boasts how quickly it can take you from nought to sixty miles per hour. A key measurement for our churches is how soon we can take people from 'feel like strangers' to 'feels like home'.

Our friend Pastor Jon Skelton does this so well. You know where his church meets by the unmissable banners showing you to the front door. Smiling faces greet you on entry and first timers get a welcome bag as they cross the threshold containing a load of goodies including a branded travel mug. More people say hello as you are shown to the coffee bar where your mug is filled and you are offered fresh pastries. By the time you take your seat, you have had several opportunities to connect with people who are genuinely interested in you, and you feel like the church had prepared for you to be there.

The welcome is especially important for first timers with children. Phil's family were on holiday recently and wanted to go to church on Sunday morning (and not preach!). The church had nailed their welcome, his two boys were registered at the door by the kids' team and shown where their group would be. As parents, we felt reassured and Caleb and Jos loved their morning learning about Jesus in a different setting. At Jon's church, someone in a giant teddy bear costume greets children with a high five (and adults too if they raise their paw!)

Every church doesn't need a bespoke mug in a gift bag or a church member in fancy dress in the car park, but each of us needs to reflect the welcome of God to everyone who walks through our doors – and many of us can grow in this area. And, as with all these EPIC features, the quality of the welcome is not dependent on the size of the church.

This is also not limited to church life but applies to our homes and entire personas. How might all of us daily embody the 'welcome home' of Jesus? We also need to remember welcoming is a team game. How might each of us play our part in making each other feel at home in every gathering of the people of God?

The living room

When Gavin and Anne wrote their book *Unleashed*, one of the emphases was on the daily expression of radical community explained by Luke in this passage in Acts 2:

They devoted themselves to the apostles' teaching and to fellowship, to the breaking of bread and to prayer. Everyone was filled with awe at the many wonders and signs performed by the apostles. All the believers were together and had everything in common. They sold property and possessions to give to anyone who had need. Every day they continued to meet together in the temple courts. They broke bread in their homes and ate together with glad and sincere hearts, praising God and enjoying the favour of all the people. And the Lord added to their number daily those who were being saved. (Acts 2:42–47)

105

For many of us, church has been somewhere we go once a week, rather than something we are every day. Some have pointed out that expecting one point of contact a week to sustain our spiritual walk is like providing dial-up internet in the age of Wi-Fi. If we are to reflect the explosive growth and wholehearted commitment of our first-century trailblazing predecessors, we will need smaller groups and strong interpersonal relationships alongside our weekly big church family gathering. Welcome to our living room, the space where friends and family sit, laugh, relax, forge friendship and learn to be comfortable in one another's presence.

One of the devastating cultural trends that we must respond to is the epidemic of loneliness in our world. Towards the end of 2023, the World Health Organization declared that loneliness was a 'global pressing health threat' and reiterated its harmful effects on our physical and mental wellbeing.[7] Phil has written extensively on the need for and importance of friendship in recent years, and it continues to be the most important, least talked about relationship in our world. But encouragingly, since the publication of *The Best of Friends*, as the volume has been turned up on the friendship conversation, churches have discovered its power in terms of deepening discipleship, enabling evangelism and fostering intergenerational and intercultural connections.[8] As Nicky Gumbel says, 'People will come to church for many reasons, but they will stay for only one – friendship.'[9]

To cultivate these vital relationships, we need to emphasise the need for smaller, living-room-sized gatherings. We tend to give a

---

7 S. Johnson, 'WHO Declares Loneliness a "Global Public Health Concern"', *The Guardian*, 16 November 2023, https://www.theguardian.com/global-development/2023/nov/16/who-declares-loneliness-a-global-public-health-concern (accessed 23 October 2024).

8 P. Knox, *The Best of Friends: Choose wisely, care well* (London: IVP, 2023).

9 C. Lodge, 'Nicky Gumbel: "People come to church for many reasons, they stay for one – friendship"', Christian Today, 6 May 2014, https://www.christiantoday.com/article/htb.leadership.conference.2014.people.come.to.church.for.many.reasons.they.stay.for.one.friendship/37220.htm (accessed 23 October 2024).

lot of thought and energy to our Sunday gathering(s), and these are important. But while these meetings are great for bringing the whole church family together for sung worship and common teaching, they are limited in helping people form meaningful relationships – no matter how good the coffee is! Churches that integrate, disciple and connect people well give thought and investment to creating spaces for authentic friendships to thrive.

The kitchen

Please forgive us if you think the link here a little tenuous. In the kitchen, we want to talk about the teaching that is served. What food is available to nourish and help grow strong disciples – and how is it being served? How are talks prepared and how are they delivered? What are the vital ingredients?

When we talk about the impact of the digital revolution and its impact on how we do church, the conversation quickly leaps to the use of technology – whether we have the latest equipment or are on the relevant social media platforms. These are of some importance but, if that is where the conversation stays, we often miss a far more subtle change that has taken place: the way we access and interact with information. And you might not realise the impact it has had on our brains.

We might not need to convince you that where you go to get what you need to know has changed. After all, to 'Google' has become one of our favourite verbs. For the digital natives reading this book, you might be astonished to discover that there was a time before smartphones where you went to the library to do your research. In this pre-digital world, Wikipedia's predecessor was the *Encyclopaedia Britannica*. It embodied how truth was communicated in the age of the printing press – through bullet points and linear reasoning. It appealed to the part of our brain wired for logic, reason and analysis – the so-called 'left brain', the bit that enjoys spreadsheets. But things have changed. The unseen shift that has taken place is that when we use the internet to access information, we enter a matrix of pages, tabs and platforms – and truth is primarily mediated through narrative, image and metaphor.[10] It appeals to the part of our brain wired for stories, poetry and creativity – the so-called 'right brain', the bit that is better at art.

This has profound implications for how we communicate. Many of us preachers began communicating in a pre-digital age, or at least when it was yet to have the pervasive impact it now has. This means our style can appeal much more to the 'left brain' way of thinking that is wired for reason. We love our propositional statements and bullet points beginning with the same letter. If we are to connect with today's culture, especially younger generations, we are going to need to balance this with increased emphasis on the 'right brain' way of thinking. We will need to exercise and grow our storytelling and poetic muscles and consider the images and metaphors that will connect timeless substance in today's style.

Jesus is an excellent role model for us. He would frequently declare propositional truths, 'I am the way, the truth and the life,' and engage in logical, analytical debate. But he was also a famous storyteller, 'A man was walking from Jerusalem to Jericho… There was a man who had two sons…' Preaching that swims with the current must appeal to the logical, analytical left brain and the creative, story-hungry right brain. We can all be more Christ-like in our communication.

The UK Church is full of very gifted, godly and powerful communicators like this. At a recent celebration of Christianity and football at Wembley Stadium, Phil watched the speaker masterfully connect stories from football to gospel truth. One friend has an extraordinary ability to use imagination to put her listeners at the heart of the biblical story. Another is an expert at finding good

---

10 See more in L. Sweet, *Viral: How social networking is poised to ignite revival* (Colorado Springs: Waterbrook Press, 2012), pp. 91–100.

news connections with everyday events that help people connect cultural cues to Christ. One of our colleagues can speak to all generations but has a particular gift for fiery preaching to young adults, communicating uncompromising gospel truth in language they understand. These examples are a drop in the ocean. All over the nations, preachers, teachers, youth and children's workers, small group leaders work hard week in week out to faithfully communicate timeless truth in a way that connects with listeners' hearts.

As those who love communicating, and know we have the best news ever for a world that desperately needs to hear it, we are always asking how we adapt our style to communicate the unchanging gospel to a changing world. Words matter. The substance matters. But let's never stop growing in our desire to communicate well – and keep on trying to hone our skills in this area.

The dining room

When we were both teenagers, you might not be surprised to find out that we were not always the best behaved. Occasionally this would mean that our parents would need to have a difficult conversation with us, and often these would take place around the dining room table. When we talked about the conversations that we have in the kitchen, we focused particularly on the style of communication. Now we are thinking about substance. Families talk about life and discuss the big issues around the table.

John Stott continually stressed the importance of 'double listening' as we ask how the Bible speaks into the conversations in the world.[11] We must listen well to both. Our encouragement from our seat at the dining room table is to make sure that we connect our faith to the everyday of our lives. We love what our friends at the London Institute of Contemporary Christianity have done in

---

11 J. Stott, *The Contemporary Christian: An urgent plea for double listening* (London: IVP, 1992).

this area and their language of whole life discipleship. This matters for Christians. We must keep connecting God to every area of our lives. It also matters for not-yet Christians. Far too often they see faith as irrelevant. When we connect the truth and wisdom of Jesus to issues they are thinking about, we demonstrate the relevance of faith to them. And sometimes this involves preaching on difficult subjects. Issues such as money, sexuality, identity, racial justice, the environment and mental health need to be talked about and grappled with.

There is also significant value in constantly thinking about themes that provoke intrigue among not-yet Christians and explaining that the Bible has beautiful wisdom that speaks to these areas of life. Our friend Leon Evans leads a church where each week, the title of the talk is advertised on social media and he finds that these talk titles frequently scratch where people are itching. Recent talks have included, 'Ever wonder why I am here?', 'How to get better at decision-making', 'How to keep your cool when angry' and 'Googling God: Does science contradict faith?' Unsurprisingly, his church is thriving among all ages and the church's YouTube channel has thousands of subscribers.

It is also worth noting that the setting for these issues is the table, a space for dialogue, not necessarily a one-way information stream. Commentators note that we have moved in the last thirty years from the age of mass media to social media, from a broadcast mindset to one of interaction and influence. The popularity of reality television means that we have become culturally acclimatised to influencing the result of what we watch. We are not suggesting people should vote to get their preferred ending to a sermon! But we do need to ask how we engage people in an age of increased participation. Biblical truth is not changed to suit the audience, but especially when we engage with difficult issues, it is important to create environments where people feel comfortable expressing their opinions and can engage in discussion around them.

We hope our 'home' is useful in helping us all think about what the Church of the future looks like. Ultimately, we long for a Church that glorifies Jesus and reaches the lost. We are encouraged by so much of what God is doing through his Church in the UK. Where it is biblically faithful, missional in heart and innovative in practice, there is always health – and healthy things grow.

But aren't we meant to be different?

Whenever we talk about being culturally relevant, there is often the pushback that we are meant to do things differently from the way the world does it. In some instances, this is true. Take communion, for example. When we go to a sporting event with friends, we each get our own lunch and drink rather than breaking off bits from one sandwich and solemnly passing it around. Many of our practices are just weird and we need to own that. And in some cases, there is a holy mystery that comes with the weirdness that attracts people and that God uses to draw people to himself. Because he is supernatural, and 'not a tame lion', God certainly acts in ways that are strange and out of the ordinary and we cannot become so relevant that we limit him in this way.

In Matthew 5–7, we read the Sermon on the Mount. Here we get a wonderful glimpse of God's kingdom way of living that is so different from our cultural understanding. It is so distinct, often surprising and utterly compelling. We are called to give up everything to follow Jesus as we seek to live out his revolutionary kingdom manifesto. When Jesus calls on us to be 'salt' and 'light' (5:13–16), this is a clear call to not blend in but to stand out, not to conform but to flavour, preserve and enlighten our landscape. Both salt and light are effective simply because they are different and people often respond to the gospel because they see the difference in us due to the Lord's work and reign in our lives. We should be influencers within our culture not the influenced. Michael Green puts it this way, 'there should be a flavour of Christlikeness, a sparkle of joy and unselfishness about them that is immensely attractive.'[12]

Interestingly, historian and author Tom Holland, looking in from outside the Church, has identified this very advantage. On an episode of *The Surprising Rebirth of Belief in God* podcast he stated, 'The area of growth seems to be churches that take the supernatural seriously... that take angels and signs from God and miracles seriously. I don't understand why anyone would be interested in a Christianity that isn't taking this stuff seriously.'[13]

Critically, we need to distinguish between doing things in a certain way because that is how they have to be done and doing things in that way because that's the way we have always done them and we lack the imagination or inclination to change. The important thing is to remove any unnecessary barrier that prevents people encountering Jesus. In Acts 15, the early church are discussing whether new believers who have come from a non-Jewish background need to be circumcised or not in order to be accepted into the Church. James, at the council meeting says these important words, 'we should not make it difficult for the Gentiles who are turning to God' (Acts 15:19).

The ancient paths

We also remember that while some human-made practices have become unhelpful and obsolete for today's church, we can benefit from 2,000 years of wisdom from those who have gone before. We are not advocating that we must rewrite the entire playbook in the name of cultural relevance. For example, there are centuries-old prayers and practices in almost every tradition that have stood the

---

12 M. Green, *The Message of Matthew* (London: IVP, 2001), p. 91.

13 J. Brierley, 'Episode 30: Surprised by God – 3 ways to welcome the returning tide of faith' [Podcast], *The Surprising Rebirth of Belief in God* podcast, https://justinbrierley. com/surprisingrebirth/episode-30-surprised-by-god-3-ways-to-welcome-the-returning-tide-of-faith/ (accessed 18 December 2024).

test of time because they contain a timeless quality and unlock something in the human heart wherever that individual stands on the timeline of eternity. Jeremiah speaks of these rhythms when he writes:

Stand at the crossroads and look;
    ask for the ancient paths,
ask where the good way is, and walk in it,
    and you will find rest for your souls.
(Jeremiah 6:16)

I, Phil, was speaking at a church in Northern Ireland recently that had begun less than a decade before with a handful of young adults. It had since grown to a thriving community of hundreds, with an average age of well under forty. This is a vibrant church, where you feel at home from the moment a coffee is offered as you walk through the door. There are many of the EPIC features we have discussed in this chapter and yet there are also hallmarks of the ancient paths. First, they have recently taken over a building in the centre of Belfast steeped in history. The previous congregation are no longer physically present, but the walls still tell some of that story. Secondly, as part of the service, there was the dedication of a small baby. In the ceremony, the pastor took the child in his arms, looked into their startled eyes and spoke over them the ancient words of Numbers 6:

The LORD bless you
    and keep you;
The LORD make his face shine upon you
    and be gracious to you;
The LORD turn his face toward you
    and give you peace.
(Numbers 6:24–26)

Then the community sang that same blessing together. At first it felt a bit weird. But it was utterly beautiful to sing together these 3,500-year-old words and commit the baby to their Creator. It was a stunning fusion of the old and new.

Not by power or might

Finally, we are not adapting alone, nor is it primarily our responsibility. Jesus said he would build his Church, but it is on Peter the rock (Matthew 16:18). Jesus declares that he is the good shepherd (John 10:11) but commissions Peter to feed his sheep (John 21:16). The invitation of belonging to God's Church is that we get to partner with him in becoming a missional community of good news people. But we must not do it all ourselves. When it comes to reimagining Church for today's generations, we must remember we have the Holy Spirit with us and his wisdom is priceless.

First, the Holy Spirit helps us discern the times. Jesus said that he would, 'lead [us] into all truth' (John 16:13) and Paul reminds us that 'The Spirit searches all things, even the deep things of God' (1 Corinthians 2:10). Against a bewildering cultural backdrop we can say with Jehoshaphat, 'We do not know what to do, but our eyes are upon you' (2 Chronicles 20:12). Second, the Holy Spirit is the ultimate source of creativity. It was the Spirit active and hovering over the waters at creation (Genesis 1:2), and the Spirit who filled the Bible's first artists Bezalel and Oholiab as they created the tabernacle (Exodus 31:1–11). Third, we know that he is always in the business of renovating the Church. Isaiah reminds us, 'See, I am doing a new thing! Now it springs up; do you not perceive it?' (Isaiah 43:19). In our partnership with him, our job is to see where the Spirit is already at work, make sure we notice it and join in.

A Blockbuster blunder

We conclude this chapter where it began, in the store where Gavin watched a young family staring at a cartoon elephant. At its peak, Blockbuster video had 9,000 stores across the globe and the business was worth 3 billion dollars. In early 2000, Netflix founders Reed Hastings and Marc Randolph flew to the Blockbuster headquarters in Dallas to offer to sell their fledgling streaming service to the rental store giant. The price was 50 million dollars. The Blockbuster executives did not see a future for streaming services. They failed to read the signs of the times.

Ten years later, Blockbuster filed for bankruptcy. Video might have killed the radio star, but streaming killed the video store. Netflix is worth rather more than their offer to Blockbuster, valued at around 300 billion dollars with over 250 million subscribers. It is a cautionary tale for those who refuse to listen to the winds of change.

Our grandparents grew up in the UK in an age where a significant proportion of the population went to church. Most people knew the basics of the Christian story. Our church gatherings and practices were set up in and for this time, just as Blockbuster was set up for an age where people had VHS machines and no high-speed broadband. The seismic cultural changes of the last century mean that the upbringing and worldviews of today's generations have very little frame of reference for who Jesus is and what happens at church. All over the UK, there are models of excellence of how local churches are responding to cultural changes. Our times call for a posture that listens to the Spirit's guidance of the Church and adapts accordingly. We need to stand on the rock of substance and adjust our stylistic sails to the cultural winds.

Taking it further

- Creating a culture where people feel at home might sound like the church leader's job. But while there might be some changes that only they can make, all of us can play a part in creating an EPIC sense of home for those around us.
  - Reflect on the four EPIC features. When you think about your church community, what do you do well? Which aspect could do with some positive change?
  - How's your hallway? How might you make people feel more welcome at church, at work, in your local community?
  - How's your living room? Are you part of smaller spaces where deep friendships can be made?
  - How's your kitchen? How creative and engaging is your communication?
  - How's your dining room? Are you able to have the difficult conversations? Are you preaching on and discussing the real issues that affect people's lives?
- Most of us are resistant to change. How open is your church community to change? When decision makers attempt to move things forward stylistically, how might you help shape that process in a positive way?
- What are the ancient paths that have brought you life? What practices – both individual and corporate – fasting, gratitude, Sabbath, communion, silence, solitude, confession – have deepened your relationship with Jesus in a superficial world?

Recommended reading

Being Human: A new lens for our cultural conversations by Jo Frost and Peter Lynas (London: Hodder & Stoughton, 2023) – A practical and engaging book that seeks to help us find our place in the cultural conversations of our day. This book offers a new lens to help us engage with the four key areas of humanity: significance, connection, presence and participation.

The Air We Breathe: How we all came to believe in freedom, kindness, progress and equality by Glen Scrivener (Epsom: The Good Book Company, 2022) – A stunning exploration of our culture's desire for the kingdom without the King. The author masterfully demonstrates how our world elevates and idolises the moral virtues of compassion, equality and consent without realising that they all find their root in Jesus.

The themes of this chapter can be explored further using small group resources, videos and discussion questions. Delve deeper at www.goodnewspeople.church

6

We need to be hopeful and realistic

'We must accept ... the finite disappointment, and yet cling to the infinite hope.'[1]
Martin Luther King Jr

One of the defining characteristics of good news people is that we are people of hope. Hopefulness flows out of all four of our evangelical firm foundations. Because we are Bibliocentric, we trust the big story of Scripture that it will all be all right in the end. Because we are cruciocentric, we can celebrate the hope of eternal life that the cross and resurrection make possible. Because we are conversionist, we embrace the reality that we are a new creation – because of our decision to follow Jesus, hope now lives in our hearts. And because we are activist, we embody and bring hope through our words and actions to our world that so desperately needs it.

As we will explore in this chapter, this posture of hopefulness is desperately needed in today's world, but we also recognise that this needs to be held in tension with a grounded realism in light of the struggles that we face as Christians and as a world. When it comes to this balance between hopefulness and realism, it can be easy to fall off the tightrope onto one side or the other.

Hopefulness without realism is just blind optimism. There is a famously funny scene in *Monty Python and the Holy Grail* where The Black Knight is stubbornly blocking King Arthur's way. During

---

1 M. L. King Jr, sermon, https://kinginstitute.stanford.edu/king-papers/documents/draft-chapter-x-shattered-dreams (accessed 17 April 2025).

the subsequent duel, the knight loses his limbs one by one but refuses to admit defeat. When his left arm is lopped off, he brushes it off as a mere scratch. Losing the right arm prompts another defiant response, claiming nothing serious has happened. Even as he's left hopping on one leg, he insists on his invincibility. Finally, reduced to just a torso and head, he grudgingly suggests that it is a stalemate as King Arthur sweeps past. We are not called to be so blindly unaware of the realities of the world around us that we pretend life is all blessing and no battle. If we project this attitude to the world, people may assume we are deluded, with our heads in the sand or the clouds, oblivious to the problems that face them and all of us.

Conversely, realism without hopefulness is unnecessary pessimism. In C. S. Lewis's *The Silver Chair*, this posture is characterised by a 'marshwiggle' called Puddleglum, the companion of Jill and Eustace on their adventure to save Prince Rillian. When we first meet him, his first questions are whether the king is dead, or if Narnia is flooded or has been attacked by dragons. When they are given a mission, his first response is to say that they are looking for a prince that probably isn't there, in a city that no one has ever seen, in the cold of winter. For him, the glass isn't half full or half empty – it's got dregs of poison in the bottom.

Your authors once played for a Monday night seven-a-side football team that was full of heart, but lacking in technical ability. We lost more games than we won but the two of us would turn up every week believing we could beat whoever we were playing. To our frustration, this was not the attitude of all our teammates, who did their best to embody the spirit of Puddleglum. One night, we were playing the team that was top of the league and, in a sincerely meant team talk, our manager uttered these immortal words before a ball had been kicked, 'Tonight, gents, I think it is probably a case of damage limitation.' Without hopefulness, we can go through life starting each day feeling defeated before we have even got out of bed.

Hope to be treasured

In this stunning passage, Paul encapsulates the tension between hope and realism as he writes to the church in Corinth:

> But we have this treasure in jars of clay to show that this all-surpassing power is from God and not from us. We are hard pressed on every side, but not crushed; perplexed, but not in despair; persecuted, but not abandoned; struck down, but not destroyed. We always carry around in our body the death of Jesus, so that the life of Jesus may also be revealed in our body.
> (2 Corinthians 4:7–10)

First, these words are deeply honest and real about our human condition. To be compared to jars of clay is as flattering as other parallels the Bible makes – between us and sheep or dust. Jars are fragile, easily cracked and broken. In Paul's day, they were cheap equivalents of glass or metal vessels. The reality check continues in the following verses. 'Hard pressed' describes the experience of many of us on a daily basis as we struggle to balance work, family, relationships, finances, church and health. As we look at the world around us, we are so often 'perplexed' by the events on our newsfeeds. We are sure that we have not been the only ones over the last few years to have asked the Lord, 'What is going on?' Verse 9 describes us as 'persecuted'. Hear us well on this: in the UK we do not suffer the same levels of oppression as some of our brothers and sisters around the world, but there is an increasing chill factor towards Bible-believing Christians in this moment. Finally, we are 'struck down'. Scholars suggest that these words are trying to communicate the emotional and mental struggle that Paul is facing.[2] He is not in a good way.

---

2 P. Barnett, *The Message of 2 Corinthians* (London: IVP, 2020), p. 88, summarises this. See also M. A. Seifrid, *The Second Letter to the Corinthians* (Nottingham: Apollos, 2014), pp. 206–7.

If you are ever hesitant to confess to a good friend that you are struggling, this honesty from the apostle Paul should encourage you to open up. We can be real with ourselves, others and God about the challenges that surround us and the effect they have on our fragile emotions. Don't let your hopefulness prevent you from being authentic before others.

However, the gospel power of this paragraph is found in its first five words, 'But we have this treasure.' The message is emphatic: if you are a Christian, that changes everything. You may be like a jar of clay, but there is treasure within. Our hearts may be fragile, but they are bursting with hope. It means we can declare with Paul that despite the pressure, confusion, persecution and depression, we are not crushed, in despair, abandoned or destroyed. That is the power of hope in Jesus.

In an age of disillusionment, politicians and advertisers alike have tried to harness the power of hope to capture our minds, vote or purchasing decisions. This can be taken to extremes. Multimillion-pound advertisements by a mainstream fast-food provider urge us to, 'Believe in chicken.' A recent Christmas marketing campaign from a company selling butter rather ambitiously claimed that, 'There is hope in baking.' We are as partial to a Victoria sponge or a custard slice as most people, but our hope is not in cakes and pastries. There is a glorious video clip that illustrates this sort of misplaced trust. The scene is a classic small group Bible study where the pastor invites a volunteer to stand on a chair in the middle of the room. He explains that the group are going to fill in and when he falls, they will catch him. The man closes his eyes and mentally prepares to put his faith in his friends. As he does, they form an arc behind him and there are more than enough to give him a safe landing. The pastor counts down: 3... 2... 1... The volunteer falls *forwards*.

Hope only has value if it is in the right direction.

In an age where there are so many things competing for our desires, resources and attention, we need to be single-minded about the direction of our hope. Our *deepest* hope is not in world peace or any form of government or politics. It is not in our next house move or promotion at work. It is not in friends and family. It certainly is not in the success of our sports team. As Christians, our deepest hope has a name, and his name is Jesus.

The power of hope

One morning, I, Phil, sleepily boarded my 6:26 am train to London and stumbled into the onboard shop for a much-needed injection of morning caffeine. There, I made the mistake of asking the barista how she was doing. Sue (clocked the name badge) replied with a tsumani of pain. She lamented a list of woes from an achy foot to the threat of a Third World War, to which I smiled sympathetically, while regretting asking the initial question. When she had finished, my response was sympathetically cheery, 'We all need a bit of hope, don't we?!' As I walked away, purchased latte in hand, her words rang in my ears, 'But there is no hope!'

Back in my table seat, I opened my laptop. The sun had not yet risen and I reflected on Sue's words and the swirling darkness outside. It caused me to ponder the link between light and hope. In a physical sense, when we are surrounded by gloom, the sight of the smallest illumination can draw us forward to believe that everything will eventually be all right. No wonder in so many places in the Bible, its authors draw similar parallels, 'The light shines in the darkness, and the darkness has not overcome it' (John 1:5).

In so many ways, as we scroll down our newsfeeds and feel the weight of the permacrisis on our shoulders, we need to embrace our role in the world as hope-bearers. This should bring great joy to us – but can also lead to a sense of responsibility for others. As I tried to concentrate on my work on the screen in front of me on the train that morning, I could not shake Sue's 'hopeless' decree, and I felt the Holy Spirit nudge me to do something about it. So, I nervously wrote her a note telling my story and why faith in Jesus gives me the hope that whatever life holds, it will all be ok in the end.

I wandered back to the on-board shop. 'Sue,' I said, 'I have been thinking about what you said about there not being any hope, and wanted to share with you that I believe that there is always hope. I've written you a note telling you my story.' I sheepishly and nervously handed it across (as mentioned, sometimes us evangelists don't feel as bold as we appear). 'I hope it encourages you and that your day is more hopeful.' Her face lit up and she appeared overwhelmed at the gesture. Hope and kindness are extraordinarily powerful.

Author and ethicist Lewis Smedes writes:

Hope is to our spirits what oxygen is to our lungs. Lose hope, and you die. They might not bury you for a while, but without hope you are dead inside. The only way to face the future is to fly straight into it on the wings of hope... hope is the energy of the soul. Hope is the power of tomorrow.[3]

The gift of hope

Back in 2 Corinthians 4, having established the 'all-surpassing power' of the treasure in our jars, Paul shifts the conversation onto what this means for how we relate to the world around us:

It is written: 'I believed; therefore I have spoken.' Since we have that same spirit of faith, we also believe and therefore speak, because we know that the one who raised the Lord Jesus from the dead will also raise us with Jesus and present us with you to himself. All this is for your benefit, so that

---

3 J. Lowther, *Kick Story: A wild ride of calling, adventures and a glorious God* (PublishU, 2024), p. 173.

the grace that is reaching more and more people may cause
thanksgiving to overflow to the glory of God.
(2 Corinthians 4:13–15)

It is almost as though the treasure is so abundant and powerful,
the container cannot contain it. The gift of faith is so good that we
have to talk about it: 'We believe and therefore speak.' As those with
treasure in our hearts, we are those who bear and bring hope to
those in our world who desperately need it. In the book's opening
pages, we introduced the concept of the 'permacrisis'. Against this
backdrop, as non-believers face life's realities in an increasingly
secular and inward-looking society, we must be those to whom our
friends look to for hope. Mark Sayers describes the hypothetical
situation of smoke filling a packed room, someone screaming,
'Fire!' and all the exits being blocked. In that scenario, people look
to the calmest person in the room who offers a way out and the
assurance that everything will be ok. This posture has become
known as a 'non-anxious presence'.[4]

The latest research backs this up. The *Finding Jesus* study shows
that the swirling chaos of the world is contributing significantly to
people looking to faith and people who bear good news.[5] When we
asked almost 300 new Christians what instigated their faith journey,
the most cited reasons were 'needing help with life', 'looking for
meaning' and 'painful/difficult experiences'.[6] The research shows
it is at this point they then turn to friends and community to help
them on their journey.

I, Gavin, remember so clearly visiting my now wife on the Wirral
when we were going out. I grew up in south-east London which
felt like it was on another planet compared with where Anne was

---

4 M. Sayers, *A Non-anxious Presence: How a changing and complex world will create a remnant of renewed Christian leaders* (Chicago: Moody, 2022).

5 *Finding Jesus* (2025).

6 *Finding Jesus* (2025).

raised. The Wirral was beautiful, operated at a slower pace, had many wide-open spaces, was surrounded with water and seemed to me to be an England I'd only seen in old television programmes. Anne was also part of a large church youth group which had been run wonderfully by volunteers for years. It was a lot of fun to get to know other members of this group and many of Anne's friends quickly became important to me too.

This was all over twenty-five years ago and fast forwarding to just a couple of years back, Anne got heartbreaking news from a friend. A fellow youth group member from yesteryear had been diagnosed with terminal cancer. She was married to another friend of ours and had a young son and daughter. The news was devastating and drove us to our knees. We believed for a miracle and had seen the Lord do so much over the years. Prayer was galvanised all over the UK and we really believed that the God who can move mountains would drive the cancer from our friend's body.

This whole journey only grew the faith of our friend and she became more and more devoted to the Lord. She was baptised and there was not a dry eye in the house as her oxygen tank was briefly removed to allow her to be fully immersed. I'd love to give a wonderful happy ending to it all but life is not always like that. When we preached together at Spring Harvest France in the summer of 2024, Anne shared some of the story. She was realistic but also profoundly hopeful about what could happen. But before we had left the campsite, she received the call she was dreading. Her friend had gone to be with Jesus.

A few weeks later, we were at her funeral. In her forty-three years of life, our friend had hugely impacted so many and this was shown by the rows of people standing at the back of the church once every seat was taken. Anne preached powerfully from Romans 8:31–39 about nothing separating us from the love of God and the truth that if God is for us, who can be against us? In a room full of mourners, Anne owned what it is to be realistic and hopeful. She shared how she, as much as anyone, had prayed, longing and groaning for a miracle. This hadn't happened and so we who are left behind need to hold on to the hope we have in Jesus. He is still good. Equally, she was realistic about the grief we were facing and how hard it is when things turn out differently to how we might have hoped. I sat there feeling challenged, impacted and comforted knowing that, somehow, in the end we can always have hope, no matter how difficult the storm. I prayed that our friend's widower and children might come to see this in time too.

The Lord never promised that life would work out how we would like. He promised to be with us in all the challenges. During those difficult days, I was struck by the fact that it was Anne the friends and family looked to. We Christians carry hope to those around us, especially in times of acute pain and need.

Where realism meets hope

The challenge for many of us is this: even though the Bible continually reminds us that we are filled with the Spirit of God (Galatians 4:6), even though this gives us the power to be witnesses of the good news (Acts 1:8), we often feel more like fragile jars of clay than vessels bursting with treasure. Sometimes we feel more 'hard pressed' than 'not crushed'. Our aching and ageing physical bodies remind many of us of this on a daily basis. The verses in 2 Corinthians go on to acknowledge this:

Therefore we do not lose heart. Though outwardly we are wasting away, yet inwardly we are being renewed day by day. For our light and momentary troubles are achieving for us an eternal glory that far outweighs them all. So we fix our eyes not on what is seen, but on what is unseen, since what is seen is temporary, but what is unseen is eternal.
(2 Corinthians 4:16–18)

When we reflect on difficult seasons of life, we often recognise God's help in seeing us through. But we also see the ways in which God has actually used our weaknesses and limitations for his glory. We have known chapters of life when we have been trying to serve God faithfully, but have been at the end of ourselves, running on fumes with personal grief and trauma lurking backstage. And often, it is these very vulnerabilities that allow God to do his best work through us. It is as if the more cracks that appear in the jar, the more the treasure has the opportunity to be seen by those looking on. It is this paradox that Paul speaks of a few chapters later when he declares that he will 'boast all the more gladly about [his] weaknesses, so that Christ's power may rest on [him]' (2 Corinthians 12:9). It is in this tension that hope and reality meet. We must be real about the painful discouragements and hardships we face, but be hopeful that in them, God is with us and is doing something in us and through us.

I, Phil, experienced this through the early months of the coronavirus pandemic. For much of 2020, it felt like my life was under siege. There was the discouragement and disappointment of my first book *Story Bearer* being published in the March of that year. After years of writing and months of preparation for a successful launch, the book was released the same week all the shops closed because of the lockdown restrictions. Then, far more tragically, the news came that my mum's cancer was terminal. I spent time each day in the following months sitting at the end of her driveway, watching her physically deteriorate. But this was a remarkable woman who had chosen to follow Jesus as a young girl. There was treasure in her gradually degrading frame. When I read verse 16 of 2 Corinthians 4, every word was true for my mum at that time. Outwardly her body was failing, and yet inwardly she had never been so spiritually strong. It was as if, throughout her life, she had invested in a spiritual bank account. In her dying days, she had deep reserves to draw from.

But the treasure could not help but spill through the cracks. In her final days, she decided to do something we would recommend to others, if we get the opportunity. One afternoon, she took her iPad and recorded a message to be played at her funeral. She was always someone who liked to have the last word. She spoke of how her decision to follow Jesus had meant she knew forgiveness for her past, God with her in her present agony, and the absolute assurance that she would go to heaven when her fragile jar of clay could no longer hold her. On 8 June 2020, her earthly body gave way. Because of the restrictions in place at the time, the large-scale in-person celebration we would have wanted was not possible, so it had to be on Zoom. Hundreds of screens turned up and there were few dry eyes as my mum's recorded message was played. I then gave the opportunity for those on the call to choose to follow Jesus.

As the adrenaline and emotion dissipated and the meeting was closed, I turned my phone back on and saw a message I had received from one of my mum's friends. Mum had prayed for her over many years. The message said simply that she had joined in with the prayer of commitment and believed that Jesus had died for her. As my mum's death approached, she knew the reality of what was to come, but she also held onto the hope of the glory ahead of her. She knew that with the little time she had left, there was still more glory she could bring to Jesus.

We will never know the answers to many of the prayers that we pray. Perhaps that is why Paul encourages us in verse 18 to fix our eyes on the eternal and the unseen. The comforts of this life can all too easily distract us from living in the light of eternity. Every generation of Christian has lived in the reassuring knowledge that whatever we face, the King will return. Between now and the end of time, however many bad things happen, however many wars take place, however many pandemics afflict us, however many incurable diseases overwhelm us, however much persecution there is, the end remains the same. On a more positive note, however many good things happen, however many renewals there are in the church, however many revivals take place, however many cures are discovered for previously incurable afflictions – and, dare we say, however many World Cups England win – the end still remains unchanged. Whatever takes place between now and the end of time, the finishing truth to this great story is so unchangeably simple… Jesus wins.

We must hold unwaveringly to this truth while still living out the middle of the story. The Calver family recently visited the Museum of the Bible in Washington, DC. There was a section dedicated to Billy Graham. Emblazoned on the wall was a truly profound and comforting quote. It said this: 'I've read the last page of the Bible, it's all going to turn out all right.'

Don't rule yourself out

We want to urge you never to rule yourself out of partnering with God in making a difference in the world. For many of us, when it comes to believing that our friends might come to know Jesus, that our communities might be transformed and our churches might grow exponentially, our realism far outweighs our hopefulness. And in human terms, there is every reason to feel this way. If our cause were merely an ideological movement seeking followers, there would be every reason for pessimism. The more we focus on the fragility of the jar, the more likely we are to believe that we could not possibly have a part to play; that God would want to use us. That is why we remember the treasure and are reminded it is not about us and all about Jesus. When this is our mindset, we recall countless examples in Scripture of God taking ordinary people in their frailty and joining with them to make an extraordinary difference.

Throughout the coronavirus pandemic, I, Gavin, never preached in a church building. However, at the Evangelical Alliance, we were keen to serve our member churches and so we recorded a couple of sermons for any of them to use within their online services. This was a small effort, but we wanted to do something even if it felt like it was little more than a drop in the ocean. One of these was used by over 500 churches and it was such a strange feeling on a Sunday when my emails, social media and phone messages were full of feedback from my ministry that day and yet I hadn't left my house for anything more than a short run. It was incredible to see the impact of technology and how the small efforts we make can be multiplied significantly for the kingdom. We want to be the kind of evangelicals who are always open-handed, who bring our little to Jesus – however seemingly insignificant it looks to us – and who ask him to use and multiply it for his glory.

We are built to be both realistic and hopeful – realistic about the limitations of the methodology available; yet hopeful of what's possible with such an amazing God on our side. It is so easy to feel a little hopeless as we look out on our cultural landscape. We are facing very choppy waters culturally and living in the face of a secular tsunami. It is vital that the Church stands firm on Scripture in this time of incredible challenge, yet also sees the profound opportunities for hope in such a landscape. The chaotic cultural context provides exciting and profound gospel opportunities. We must seek to understand the cultural stories shaping our world, while offering the truly good news of Jesus in the midst of economic and social turmoil. If ever there was a time to be both hopeful and realistic, then that time is surely now!

The Lord is always at work when we step up and speak out. We are reminded of Peter in Acts 2: having been filled with the Holy Spirit he stands up and speaks to the crowd, sharing the truth of the gospel. His bold declarations cause the number of early believers to go from 120 to 3,000 in just one day (Acts 2:14–41)! His hopeful disposition led him to speak up in the first place.

A realistic and hopeful Church

Hope and realism are vital for us as individuals, but we must also hold them corporately in our local communities of faith as well as a UK-wide and even as a global church.

In a recent study we conducted, young people in the UK were asked what they felt positively and negatively about. They described feeling hopeful about their immediate future, the here and now – for example, what they were having for lunch. But they were anxious and fearful about the big picture – the environment, global wars and their job prospects. In contrast, we wonder whether we evangelicals can be the opposite – optimistic about the long-term prospects and our eternal future, but worried about our imminent circumstances.

One of our aims in writing this book is to tell some of the stories of what God is doing across the UK at the moment. There are so many churches that are growing and significant numbers of people choosing to follow Jesus. But we are also aware that in your situation, you might be less than encouraged. While globally the number of Christians is expected to rise from its current number of 2.6 billion to 3.3 billion by 2050, the picture in the UK can feel a mixed bag of optimism and discouragement.[7] We must remain hopeful of renewal, and yet realistic that the picture in our weekly congregations can often seem unchanging.

Both of us are big football fans. Phil is blessed to support the much more successful Aston Villa. I, Gavin, am no less dedicated to my beloved AFC Wimbledon, but I do find myself needing to be more realistic. Villa fans can hope to hear the Champions League theme tune, but for Wimbledon, we just hope not to lose our best players or have those on loan recalled early. However, Wimbledon

---

7 Z. Dawes Jr, 'Global Christian Population Projected to Reach 3.3 Billion by 2050', Good Faith Media, 13 February 2023, https://goodfaithmedia.org/global-christian-population-projected-to-reach-3-3-billion-by-2050 (accessed 19 December 2024).

fans do love the close season when things feel more hopeful. After all, you can't lose if you're not playing! But this misses the point: football is designed to be played. In the same way, the Church is supposed to be alive and active, not hidden away in its own version of a close season.

In my role leading the Evangelical Alliance, I, Gavin, have the immense privilege of seeing some of the most exciting and significant things taking place in the UK Church. It is an honour and a delight. Equally, I am not immune to or unaware of the other side. I recently rang around thirty church leaders who had cancelled their church membership with us. I wanted to hear first-hand what the issues were and do all I could to learn and change where needed. These phone calls where not what I had expected. I thought most would have changed theologically and not liked our orthodox position on Christian marriage. This was not the case at all. One church had cancelled their membership because we were too loud on the issue and another because we were too quiet on it. However, twenty-eight of the churches had cancelled their membership as they were closed or closing. One church had gone into the pandemic with twelve people and a boiler and had sadly lost members of their congregation in that time and the boiler had broken. Another pastor wept over the phone as I prayed for him, knowing the next Sunday would be the last meeting of the church he planted forty years ago, because they were now down to eleven members and all of them were elderly.

The Church is changing in the UK. It feels like it used to be more of a set menu but is now becoming a buffet. There is much innovation taking place. In twenty-five years of ministry, I have never known so much church planting and entrepreneurial mission happening. For every church that is closing, people are starting churches. However, in the midst of all the joy, new life and hopeful stories, we want to remember those for whom this is a really hard season and things are profoundly challenging. That is what it really means to be hopeful and realistic.

Setting impatient and ambitious human goals can lead to disillusionment. Business consultant and author Jim Collins describes what he calls the Stockdale paradox. Admiral Jim Stockdale was a high-ranking American military officer held in a Vietnamese prisoner-of-war camp for eight years and the de-facto leader of the other USA captives. After surviving horrendous conditions and being tortured multiple times, he was asked which of his fellow soldiers *didn't* survive. His answer was surprising. 'The optimists,' he said. They were so convinced they would be liberated by the first Christmas that when that date came and went, they lost their resolve to live. It turns out that the phrase, 'It's the hope that kills you,' can literally be true.

But Collins also surmises from Stockdale that vital to his survival was 'an unwavering faith in the endgame.'[8] It was the duality of hope and realism that is encapsulated in the admiral's mentality:

You must never confuse faith that you will prevail in the end – which you can never afford to lose – with the discipline to confront the most brutal facts of your current reality, whatever they may be.[9]

It is Collins's observation that this paradox is a core feature of thriving organisations and we believe it is a posture that we must cling to as the body of Christ in this season. Furthermore, if this is a tension that secular movements and businesses can inhabit, how much more should we the Church hold onto it? We are those who live as bearers of the greatest hope the world has ever known. In light of this, we hold in tension the undying dream of revival, with unprecedented numbers of people turning to Jesus, alongside

8 J. Collins, *Good to Great: Why some companies make the leap... and others don't* (London: Random House Business Books, 2001), pp. 83–7.

9 J. Collins, 'The Stockdale Paradox', https://www.jimcollins.com/concepts/Stockdale-Concept.html (accessed 19 December 2024).

the surrender to the reality that it will happen in his timing. We are reminded in 2 Peter 3:9 that, 'The Lord is not slow in keeping his promise, as some understand slowness. Instead he is patient with you, not wanting anyone to perish, but everyone to come to repentance.'

Perhaps this is why God has given the Church such a diversity of optimists and pessimists. Part of our gift to one another is the balance that each of us brings in this regard. In churches, especially in leadership teams, elderships and church councils, we need pragmatists to ensure that dreamers are grounded in the detail and reality of how we get things done. But we also need 'can-do' visionaries to lift the eyes of sceptics to the possibilities in God's economy.

The garden of hope

Most of us want to be more hopeful. Even those with the most negative of attitudes do not aspire to be more pessimistic. So, the natural question arises, how do we become more hope-filled? You might think that hopefulness grows by a gradual improvement in circumstances – that as things get better, we become more optimistic of the future to come. But the Bible suggests something different.

First, it seems that our hopes for what is ahead are established by continually recalling God's faithfulness through what has been in the past. The writer to the Hebrews encourages us to 'hold unswervingly to the hope we profess, for he who promised is faithful' (Hebrews 10:23). We can trust that it all ends well because the God of the future is the same dependable God of the past. In the very next chapter of Hebrews, the author emphasises the important link between hope and faith: 'Now faith is confidence in what we hope for and assurance about what we do not see' (Hebrews 11:1). Sixteen heroes of the Bible are then mentioned in the story of

God's faithfulness from generation to generation of those who have trusted in him. In the garden of hope, we can trust that the seasons ahead will bear fruit because its fertile soil has always produced a bountiful harvest. We grow in hope not by merely staring into an assured future, but by looking back and relentlessly reminding ourselves of the chapters already written in our collective story.

Second, and even more counter-intuitively, we grow in hope for the future as we battle through the pain of our present. We have explored how our fragility and weakness often result in God making a difference through us. But it is also through our frailties and challenges that God often does an even more important work in us. Paul alludes to this in the 2 Corinthians passage, 'Though outwardly we are wasting away, yet inwardly we are being renewed day by day,' (2 Corinthians 4:16). He states it even more emphatically in Romans 5: 'Not only so, but we also glory in our sufferings, because we know that suffering produces perseverance; perseverance, character; and character, hope' (Romans 5:3–4). It would seem that one of the only ways to become more hopeful is to endure the suffering that comes with the challenges of life and the cost of following Jesus. Perhaps one of the reasons we lack resilience and hopefulness in our society is that we have become so materially and socially comfortable. As we have tried to insulate ourselves from pain, hardship and awkwardness, the cost has been the lack of opportunity to grow in emotional and spiritual toughness.

Conversely, when we encounter resilient people, they almost always have a backstory of coming through significant adversity. When we think of leaders who we know that embody character, trust, humility and ability to endure, they have often experienced deep personal tragedy, betrayal, trauma or loss. Not only have they lived to tell the tale, but it has been those circumstances that have formed them into the hopeful people they are today. In the garden of hope, it is the most difficult conditions that bear the finest fruit. And this truth is reflected throughout the natural world. Vines that grow in harsh conditions help produce grapes that can be made into the priciest of wines. Muscle is built by the hard work of tearing the tissues under great stress. As our bodies repair themselves, they overcompensate, meaning that the fibres grow back stronger so that they will be able to endure greater strain the next time they are tested. Diamonds, too, are formed under pressure.

Be more Puddleglum

We began this chapter by casting C. S. Lewis's character of Puddleglum as the archetypal pessimistic realist. However, as the adventure unfolds in *The Silver Chair*, we discover that the marshwiggle beautifully embraces and embodies the tension we have been exploring in this chapter. At a critical moment where the adventurers are in danger of falling into the enchantment of the evil queen of the Underworld, Puddleglum plunges his foot into the fire to break the magic. He remembers Aslan and the hope of Narnia and stirs his companions:

I'm on Aslan's side even if there isn't any Aslan to lead it. I'm going to live as like a Narnian as I can even if there isn't any Narnia. So, thanking you kindly for our supper, if these two gentlemen and the young lady are ready, we're leaving your court at once and setting out in the dark to spend our lives looking for Overland. Not that our lives will be very long I should think; but that's a small loss if the world's as dull a place as you say.[10]

So, this is your invitation to be hopeful realists. May we collectively believe that revival is at our doorstep, but may we also confront the brutal facts of the real challenges we face as individuals, as a Church

10 C. S. Lewis, *The Silver Chair* (London: Lions, 1980), p. 145.

and as a world. May we never underestimate the gift of hope that we carry to the world, and may we allow our hardships to build a godly resilience and reservoir of hopefulness for the days ahead.

Taking it further

- Reflect on your role as a bearer of hope. Who in your life looks to you as a non-anxious presence? Are there ways in which you are underestimating the role you could play in other people's lives?
- Consider the balance between unbridled optimism and anchored pessimism. What part do you play among your circles of friends? Think about the people you spend most time with and the voices you listen to. Do you hear too much optimism or too much pessimism?
- Ask the Lord to reveal the ways in which you have become too comfortable. Consider what you need to do to step out of your comfort zone in order to build the resilience and hopefulness you need for the season ahead.

Recommended reading

A Non-anxious Presence: How a changing and complex world will create a remnant of renewed Christian leaders by Mark Sayers (Chicago: Moody, 2022) – An exposition of the power of bringing Christ-like calm into our relationships and networks, which are characterised by chaos and constant change. As we explored in this chapter, amidst the hopelessness, those around us are looking for people who bring peace.

Where Is God in All the Suffering? by Amy Orr-Ewing (Epsom: The Good Book Company, 2020) – A powerful book that can help us find the Lord in the midst of so many struggles globally as well as pain and grief near to home. Teaches us how we can accept the reality of suffering and discover the Lord more profoundly through it.

The themes of this chapter can be explored further using small group resources, videos and discussion questions. Delve deeper at www.goodnewspeople.church

7

We need to go for decisions and make disciples

> But making disciples is far more than a programme. It is the mission of our lives. It defines us. A disciple is a disciple maker.
> Francis Chan[1]

When I, Gavin, worked at Youth for Christ, one of the highlights was getting to speak to young men in young offenders' institutes where you would meet many who were desperately looking for hope. Though these youth prisons could be intimidating, one of the great advantages of preaching there was that you always got a good crowd because the lads would get longer out of their cells if they went to chapel. If they responded to your message, they would get even longer out of their cell while they were being prayed with. This meant that every time you spoke, you got the greatest of responses. If you had gone in thinking that you had lost your evangelistic touch, you would leave believing you were the next Billy Graham! It was hard at times to know quite how much impact you were having on these lives as every time you went in to speak, every young man would respond to your message. Evangelism is shallow and shortsighted when it is solely about getting people to put their hands in the air with no follow-up, no support and no next steps on the journey of faith.

Conversely, we can become so averse to communicating the gospel that we never encourage people to make decisions. My,

---

1 F. Chan, 'A Time to Make Disciples', Relevant, 15 December 2012, https://relevantmagazine.com/faith/time-make-disciples-0/ (accessed 20 November 2024).

Phil's, first role at the Evangelical Alliance was as head of mission to young adults. I would regularly speak to rooms of church leaders, facilitating conversations about effective ministry among 18–30s. On one occasion, at a training day for around twenty clergy, I spoke about the prevailing culture, the discipleship journeys of young adults and the common ways in which they were becoming Christians. At the end of the session, a vicar approached me and said, 'I've been in my church for over thirty years. We've never really thought about doing any outreach. Maybe it's time for some evangelism.'

Jesus' ministry contained both these vital components. From the outset of his public activity, he called people to 'Repent and believe the good news' (Mark 1:15) and 'Come, follow me' (Mark 1:17). Jesus was purposeful about asking people to choose him. At the same time, his mission was characterised by teaching and a demonstration of God's power that formed those in his presence. The disproportionate amount of time he spent with the Twelve, as their rabbi, shows his intention to craft them further into his image, that they might become more like him and replicate his kingdom activity. As we identified in Chapter 2, we evangelicals are shaped by being cruciocentric and conversionist. Both these characteristics invite us to adopt a posture that is passionate about decisions made for Jesus' disciples becoming more like him.

In this chapter we want to explore the 'how' as well as the 'why' and encourage you with where God is on the move in these areas in the UK Church. We have found that growing churches regularly encourage people to become Christians and they relentlessly invite Jesus-followers further on the discipleship journey. They are deep and wide. We want to encourage you to keep asking, 'What does this mean for me?' Some of the ideas are more applicable for the whole church, but most have implications for individuals too.

How are people becoming Christians in the UK at the moment?

We want to begin this section by sharing the common themes we are seeing in the lives of those coming to faith and the practices of the churches that are helping to make this happen. These themes come from us regularly asking the question, 'What's your story?' to recent converts and 'How are you seeing people become Christians?' to church leaders. We regularly commission significant research pieces and we host the Evangelism Advisory Group, an Evangelical Alliance thinktank that regularly gathers missiologists from across the breadth of the UK Church to discuss these principles. We hope that as we share these, you are inspired by the stories, but you are also encouraged to think how you might maximise these opportunities in your witness to those around you.

Friendship

We are card-carrying proclamation evangelists. We love giving people the opportunity to decide to follow Jesus. But we are far from the most significant human influence in someone becoming a Christian. According to the research, for those who did not grow up in Christian families, the greatest impact usually comes from a friend, a neighbour, a colleague or a family member.[2] Both *Talking Jesus* (2015 and 2022) and *Finding Jesus* (2024) corroborate the importance of friendship when we ask people about who and what made a difference in their conversion stories.[3]

Why has friendship become such an important factor? First, you might argue that God has always done his best work by drawing people to himself through relationship. Some of Jesus' disciples

---

2 See *Talking Jesus* (2022), pp. 24–33.

3 *Talking Jesus* (2015 and 2022), https://talkingjesus.org/ (accessed 25 March 2025), and *Finding Jesus* (2025), www.findingjesus.co.uk

met the Son of God because their connections introduced them. After his decision to follow Jesus, Philip finds Nathanael and invites his friend to 'Come and see' (John 1:46). But the importance of friendship in recent years has been amplified because the nature of who we trust has changed.

Until relatively recently, experts were largely trusted. Over the last century in particular, the reputation of institutions and authority figures has diminished significantly. In 2023, just 9% of the UK population trusted politicians to tell the truth.[4] This has important implications for faith-sharing. The iconic image of evangelism in the twentieth century is arguably Billy Graham standing in the pulpit, Bible in hand and fire in heart. Millions flooded forward in football stadia and town halls in response to his gospel message. We still believe in this kind of proclamation, but we all need to recognise that its influence has changed with the dynamics of who we trust.

The philosopher Charles Taylor has observed that in the Western world, we have largely moved from a culture of authority to one of authenticity. This means as a society we are less inclined to want to do as we are told by those with positional power and more inclined to follow truth wherever we find it. But it also means that when exploring faith, we are far more likely to look to others who we perceive as living authentically than those in authority. This is bad news for the 'professional evangelist' but great news for friendship.

The theory and the research are reflected in the conversations we are having. In almost every story of someone we have spoken to who has come to faith as an adult, there was a friend or a family member involved in the journey. I, Phil, was speaking at a baptism service recently where an older woman shared her testimony before being baptised. She spoke of how the key relationship in bringing

---

4 M. Clemence and L. King, 'Trust in Politicians Reaches Its Lowest Score in 40 Years', Ipsos, 14 December 2023, https://www.ipsos.com/en-uk/ipsos-trust-in-professions-veracity-index-2023 (accessed 23 October 2024).

her to this point had been her daughter, who sat in the front row, her face full of grateful tears.

The challenge is that, even though relationship is one of our most effective pathways, friendships between Christians and non-Christians are in decline. In 2015, 67% of non-Christians knew a practising Christian. In 2022, that had fallen to 53%. And 46% of Christians do not know a non-Christian well enough to invite them to church. Our encouragement is to invest in your friendships, with both Christians and non-Christians, and do not miss the opportunity to invite your non-Christian friends to take the next step.

Mercy ministry and gospel

As we explored in Chapter 1, we evangelicals are passionate about loving our neighbour, and just about every one of the thousands of churches connected to the Evangelical Alliance in membership are engaged in making a tangible difference to their communities.

We have observed that these activities can play a significant role in the first rung on the ladder of many people becoming Christians. For many, their first point of contact with a church is the foodbank, debt-counselling ministry, sports programme, soup kitchen, youth provision or holiday club. The latest research tells us that 'needing help with life' was the most-cited answer when new Christians were asked about the starting point of their faith journey.[5] We asked the pastor of one rapidly growing church what the 'silver bullet' was to the growth in new believers. He replied that at his well-attended toddler group, he 'worked the room' and invited every parent, carer and family to take the next step closer to Jesus. Everyone received an invitation to an evangelistic course or the Sunday service.

In 2020, The Message Trust began a drop-in grocery in the

---

5 *Finding Jesus* (2025).

community where they are based.[6] People paid a small membership fee and came each day to get the food they needed. But each one was also invited to Alpha at the checkout. So many attended the course that a new church has started there with over 200 now attending each week.

Just recently, I, Gavin was booked to speak at a church up in the north-east of England. A few weeks before, the leader had explained that it would be great if I could arrive forty-five minutes earlier and preach twice as there were now two congregations. During the coronavirus pandemic, a couple of church members had started a local initiative to give away packed lunches to those going without food. This eventually led to a new church being formed, with many people becoming Christians through this ministry. This new congregation was full of the broken, those recently saved, some not long out of prison and many others who society had forgotten.

I was so challenged. The room smelt, the crowd wouldn't listen for long and, due to some safeguarding regulations, the service had to be finished in time for some of these folks to leave before there were under 18s around. And yet, this is where Jesus would have been – among the needy and broken. As we sang about our sins being forgiven and us being set free, it felt so authentic. It was a joy to be in the space. It was even a little disappointing when I was whisked off to share with the more conventional Sunday service meeting in the other end of the building. Mercy ministry and the gospel really can go hand in hand!

Every day, millions receive an expression of the love of God through encountering the kindness of his people. How might we ensure that we don't miss the opportunity for each one of these to hear the gospel? The joint reality of a cost-of-living crisis and our increasingly disconnected society is elevating the needs of those

---

6 The Message Trust, https://www.message.org.uk/

in our communities for both resources and relationships. What we are noticing is that where people are fed spiritually as well as physically, this is contributing significantly to the growth of the Church.

It is worth noting that historically there has been some debate about whether social action or evangelism are more important to evangelicals, especially over the course of the last century. This featured prominently at a large, historic, global gathering of evangelicals in Lausanne in 1974. The conclusion was that there should never have to be a choice between social action and evangelism, but if there ever was, evangelism should take precedence. This conversation continues today and featured significantly at the fourth Lausanne Congress held in Seoul in October 2024. A statement was released from this gathering, capturing the tension between social action and evangelism in a way that sparked further conversation and engagement.[7] We see an increasingly close relationship between the two over the coming years and want to urge the Church to maximise the opportunities presented by the amazing response of the Church to social need in the UK.

The Bible

When we explored the core elements of evangelical faith in Chapter 1, two of the segments of Bebbington's quadrilateral were the centrality of the Bible and the need for conversion. We should not be surprised that these two combine when we consider the ways in which people are becoming Christians.

Hebrews 4:12 tells us that, 'the word of God is alive and active. Sharper than any double-edged sword, it penetrates even to dividing soul and spirit, joints and marrow; it judges the thoughts and attitudes of the heart.' Throughout history, the Bible has drawn

---

7 'The Fourth Congress: The Seoul Statement', Lausanne, https://lausanne.org/statement/the-seoul-statement (accessed 23 October 2024).

people to the heart of God. Founder of Methodism, John Wesley, recalled a key moment in his conversion when he felt his heart 'strangely warmed' as he heard Martin Luther's preface to the book of Romans being read out loud.[8] The actor David Suchet became a Christian after picking up a Bible in a hotel room,[9] former vicar of Holy Trinity Brompton and pioneer of the Alpha Course, Nicky Gumbel, decided to follow Jesus at university after reading the New Testament.[10]

The pastor of a church plant told us the story of a couple who had recently joined their church. When he asked them about their journey, they said they had been talking at home about what life was really about. They had no religious background but felt compelled to pick up a Bible. They found its pages so captivating that they investigated further and ended up at church. In our research, when adults who had become Christians in the last five years were asked what caused them to finally decide to follow Jesus, the second most popular answer was 'Reading the Bible.'[11] And we should be encouraged by articles such as the one in *The Times*, which reported that Bible sales increased by 87% between 2019 and 2024, another marker point that faith is stirring across the UK.[12]

It is not surprising that in countries seeking to restrict the spread of the Christian faith, Bibles are banned. If you have friends and neighbours in your life who you are praying for to know Jesus for themselves, we would encourage you to buy them a Bible. You

---

8 J. Wesley, *Journal* (ed. N. Curnock), 24 May 1738.

9 A. Cole, 'Poirot, Prayer and the Faith of David Suchet', Evangelical Alliance, https://www.eauk.org/idea/poirot-prayer-and-the-faith-of-david-suchet.cfm (accessed 23 October 2024).

10 N. Gumbel, 'If You Want to Learn Resilience, Look to Jesus', Premier Christianity, 14 June 2023, https://www.premierchristianity.com/opinion/nicky-gumbel-if-you-want-to-learn-resilience-look-to-jesus/15742.article (accessed 23 October 2024).

11 *Finding Jesus* (2025).

12 K. Burgess, 'Spiritual Gen Z Drive Increase in Bible Sales', *The Times*, https://www.thetimes.com/uk/religion/article/spiritual-gen-z-drive-increase-in-bible-sales-vnphxfjn5 (accessed 27 March 2025).

might also offer to read it with them. When non-Christians were asked where they would go to find out more about the Christian faith, reading the Bible was second only to a Google search.[13] As Christians we can have confidence that not only does the Bible give us a cohesive, compelling and beautiful story to live by for ourselves, but we also need to be regularly reminded of how powerful it is in speaking for itself into the lives of those who have never read it before.

Digital

The average UK user spends four hours and fourteen minutes on their phone every day.[14] We touch our phones 2,617 times a day.[15] Sit on any mode of public transport, stand at any railway station or airport and most people will be staring at a screen. Other people have offered helpful commentary on the blessings and curses of the smartphone era – our observation is the increasing role the digital world is playing in many people's journey to faith.

Here are some findings from the research.[16] When non-Christians were asked where they would go to find out about the Christian faith, the top result was Google. When Christians were asked how they had come to follow Jesus for themselves, 6% said 'Attending an online church service other than a wedding or funeral.' And 4% said, 'Christian content shared on social media by people you know.' These may seem like small numbers, but they are incredibly significant when you consider that the sample included all Christians of all ages and stages of faith, the vast majority of

---

13 *Talking Jesus* (2022).

14 'Average Daily Mobile Usage in the United Kingdom from 2019 to 2023', Statista, https://www.statista.com/statistics/1285042/uk-daily-time-spent-mobile-usage/ (accessed 19 December 2024).

15 M. Winnick, 'Putting a Finger on Our Phone Obsession', Dscout, https://dscout.com/people-nerds/mobile-touches#:~:text=People%20tapped%2C%20swiped%20and%20clicked,the%20less%20restrained%20among%20us (accessed 23 October 2024).

16 *Talking Jesus* (2022), p. 32.

whom would have grown up in Christian families or become Christians as children or teenagers.

If we consider those who started to follow Jesus as adults and did not grow up in Christian families, the influence of digital content becomes very important indeed. The streaming of church services online only began on a meaningful scale in the last five years. Online church is having an extraordinary impact. Respected futurologist Patrick Dixon comments,

It's almost impossible these days to become a Christian without being profoundly influenced online. Almost every single person who has found faith in Christ in the last three years has been deeply impacted by the online ministry of your churches or other churches.[17]

How is this happening? One pathway is undoubtedly that those curious about faith in general, or a particular church, are taking a look online before turning up in person. Those of us who have been lifelong churchgoers can tend to underestimate how daunting it feels for many to cross the threshold of the doors of a place of worship. I, Phil, preached at a church in the West Midlands recently and was told about a young man called Kiran. He grew up with a diverse cultural background with a Sikh mum and a Muslim dad. His work colleague was a Christian and one day she shared the online service she had attended on her Facebook page. Kiran stumbled across it, was intrigued and listened to the talk. 'Every single time I listened to [the preacher], the things he talked about were as if he were talking to me directly,' he said. So, he began to pray and read the Bible. In his own words: 'It got profound within

---

myself.' He was invited to an Alpha course and has since become a Christian. The pastor of this church describes the streaming of Sundays as 'the row behind the back row.' It gives seekers the opportunity to take a look at what happens in an alien environment with no risk or awkwardness before they take the step to turn up in person.

A second pathway is more incidental, as people 'stumble across' Christian content on their social media platforms. Over the last few years, if you are a social media user, you may have noticed changes to the ways in which your newsfeed is populated. In the early years of a platform like Instagram, you only saw the updates of those people you followed. Now, to encourage us to keep our eyeballs fixated on their apps, designers have developed algorithms to send us content that they think we will like, based on our preferences. The more we watch videos of a certain type, the more they will send us.

This means that content will pop up that we might not expect. And for some non-Christians, occasionally this is Christian content: a clip of a preacher, spoken word, thought for the day, worship song or short gospel presentation. And this may lead to intrigue and exploration, which means the algorithm sends them more videos of this nature. The sheer volume of time people are spending on Facebook, Instagram, X and TikTok, and their power to hold our attention mean that thousands of hours of Christian content finds its way under the eyes and thumb tips of not-yet Christians. We believe that in some cases, the Holy Spirit is at work in this, and prolonged viewing is leading some to explore next steps in faith. One pastor told us, 'I've had more unchurched people come to church in the last six months through TikTok than through personal invitation.'

So how can we respond to this? First, we would suggest sharing content that you stumble across online that you think might help your friends think about life and faith. This might be your church's online service, a short clip of a talk or a clip of produced Christian media. Especially around Christmas and Easter there are some outstanding pieces of media released by Christian organisations and churches. These can inspire and provoke people to think more deeply wherever they are on the journey of faith. This is what Kiran's colleague did and it led to his life being transformed.

Second, we would suggest occasionally and appropriately 'name dropping' Jesus into what you post online or sharing something positive that your church is doing. Almost every church we know is doing something to bless its community in some way and celebrating this online can help counteract some of the negative stereotypes or preconceptions our friends may have.

Third, you might like to consider going further to use your social media platform to broadcast your story or invite those online to an evangelistic event. During lockdown, I, Phil ran an online Alpha course on Zoom with my wife Dani. Before the course started, we recorded a short video inviting our friends to join in wherever they lived or wherever they were on the journey of faith. Incredibly, friends turned up from Canada and Scotland, as well as those who lived more locally. We can often underestimate the reach and the impact we might have.

The digital world is not going anywhere. Just as the gospel spread for the early church, along the newly built Roman roads, in the years to come we foresee millions being influenced by the good news travelling along the information superhighway.

Encounter, prayer and dreams

The final theme we see is the most humbling and perhaps encouraging. More than at any other time we can remember, people are becoming Christians without any human intervention. In most cases, mission and evangelism are a partnership between us and God. The Holy Spirit is always at work in the world. His invitation to us is to join in with his divine action in the world. The most-cited response when new Christians were asked what finally made you decide to become a Christian was, 'An experience of God.'[18] And when we talk to church leaders about the ways in which people are becoming Christians at the moment, one surprising story that we are hearing is the role of dreams and people turning up at church having felt drawn in by a supernatural force. It is as if in some cases, Jesus is reminding us that he is the best evangelist.

This was my, Phil's, experience on the most recent Alpha course that I helped host. To inspire and equip the church to invite their friends, a whole teaching series took place on evangelism. It was well publicised through social media and Christmas services. On a cross at the front of church, the names of over 100 people we prayed would attend were written on sticky notes. I prepared for revival. On the first night there were just a handful of unchurched guests.

Three weeks into the course, still a little discouraged by numbers, the team met to pray before the evening started. As they did, a few unfamiliar faces walked through the door. They had somehow heard an Alpha course was happening and walked five miles on a cold January night to be there. As we got to know them, it was clear the Spirit of God had brought them to us. As they got to know Jesus, they decided to surrender their lives to him. They were baptised later that year. For all the human efforts and plans, the most fruitful activity was not our own.

We regularly hear stories like this. At one church, a university student turned up on the church steps explaining he had woken with an overwhelming burden to 'repent'. At another, an older woman told the story of how she had sensed God beckoning her to walk into the doors of the church in her village each time she passed it. When she finally gave in, she was blown away by the welcome she received from the church and from Jesus. At one church we

---

18 *Finding Jesus* (2025).

were preaching at recently, one of us asked a man on the front row how long he had been following Jesus. 'Less than a year,' he said. 'I was on holiday in Portugal and was just stood outside a shop and had an overwhelming encounter with Jesus.' He continued, 'It was so real. So powerful. I couldn't explain it so when I got home I found a church online, turned up and met the pastor. He helped me understand the gospel. I was baptised two weeks ago.'

We should be humbled by this because it reminds us that God is doing much of the work without us. At the same time, we should be inspired by these stories, first, to pray that they happen more often. Especially with friends and family members for whom we have been praying for years, perhaps a breakthrough moment might be through a dream or another supernatural intervention. Second, these moments teach us that God is always at work in the world by his Spirit. Theologians see this as part of *missio Dei*, the mission of God: the idea that God is already on mission all around us, renewing all things. Our calling is to see where he is at work and join in. Jesus recognised this in relationship to the Father: 'Very truly I tell you, the Son can do nothing by himself; he can do only what he sees his Father doing, because whatever the Father does the Son also does' (John 5:19). Finally, it should cause us to celebrate and say, 'More, Lord.' We often get things wrong, in evangelism as in life, and God is still growing his church despite us.

Good soil

These themes are far from exhaustive. In this season, we are so encouraged by the myriad ways that people are meeting Jesus for the first time or returning home to a lapsed faith. We must celebrate and learn from these and continue to prioritise evangelism but hold this in tension with the readiness to help newborn Christians grow to maturity.

Jesus was all too aware of the dangers of over-emphasising

decisions at the expense of discipleship. In the Parable of the Sower, of the four places on which the seed lands, it begins to grow in three of them (Mark 4:1–20). However, in only one of these locations does the seed end up growing into a plant that bears fruit. You might use this distribution to argue that for most human hearts, the primary challenge is not that the gospel fails to initially take root, but that it falters when confronted with opposition and the cost of following Jesus. The philosopher and author Dallas Willard could hardly place greater emphasis on the need for discipleship:

> The greatest issue facing the world today, with all its heartbreaking needs, is whether those who, by profession or culture, are identified as 'Christians' will become disciples – students, apprentices, practitioners – of Jesus Christ, steadily learning from him how to live the life of the kingdom of the heavens into every corner of human existence.[19]

Our comprehensive thoughts on how we make disciples are well beyond the remit of this book, but against the current cultural backdrop, here are a few areas we perceive the need to press into as good news people.

A churchless faith?

It is increasingly difficult to cover our ears to the deafening noise of individualism. If we allow the world to make disciples of us, this will be our inevitable destination. Our phones beckon us to customise our home screens and social media profiles around our unique personality. The 'selfie' is a perfect product of our age and was popularised by the release of the iPhone 4 in 2010 which included a front-facing camera. Why take photos of others, when your camera

19 D. Willard, *The Great Omission: Reclaiming Jesus' essential teachings on discipleship* (Oxford: Monarch Books, 2006), p. xv.

can swivel to your own portrait, and be filtered to display your features to a waiting world in a social media ecosystem? And from cars to kitchens, playlists to patios, holidays to hamburgers, we are relentlessly being offered the opportunity to tailor our experiences and purchases to suit our precious individual desires, to 'have it our way'. The writer David Foster Wallace observed of this trend, 'Everything in my immediate experience supports my deep belief that I am the absolute centre of the universe, the realest, most vivid person in existence.'[20]

Alongside this narrative sits the related pervasive value of consumerism: the concept that the free choice of consumers should drive what manufacturers create and provide to an informed market. Over the last century in particular, sociologists have noticed a shift in people's cultural mindset: rather than viewing themselves as producers of or contributors to society, they see themselves as consumers of it. The millennial generation are described as the first 100% consumer generation.[21] One commentator observes that the mantra of modernity was Descartes' *'Cogito, ergo sum'* – 'I think, therefore I am'; today's mantra is *'Tesco, ergo sum'* – 'I shop, therefore I am.'[22]

It is imperative that we are aware of the effect of these worldviews upon the way we grow as disciples, especially in relation to church. Individualism shamelessly cultivates the dangerous notion that we can be an apprentice of Jesus without the mutual friendship of, support of, encouragement of, accountability to, service to and love for others. Consumerism evokes feelings of dissatisfaction whenever our needs aren't met by a church service or community. We 'church-shop' when we get bored and say things like, 'I didn't

---

20 D. F. Wallace, *This Is Water: Some thoughts, delivered on a significant occasion, about living a compassionate life* (London: Little, Brown, 2009), p. 36.

21 S. Savage, S. Collins-Mayo, B. Mayo, with G. Cray, *Making Sense of Generation Y: The world view of 16-25-year-olds* (London: Church House Publishing, 2006), p. 144.

22 S. Hollinghurst, *Mission Shaped Evangelism: The gospel in contemporary culture* (Norwich: Canterbury Press, 2010), p. 37.

get much out of the worship today.' We often wonder whether in response to this Jesus says, 'I didn't realise it was for you.'

At our worst, our faith becomes so personal we believe we can do it on our own or we see church as a service provider. But at our best, we are aware of the harmful consequences of expressive individualism and consumerism; we commit wholeheartedly to the unstoppable, unbreakable family of God with all its expressions and expectations, rhythms and relationships, fractures and foibles and quirks and questions. We do so because we know that to be an apprentice of Jesus requires the pain, gain, grit and glory of being part of a local community of believers. Author Daniel Grothe puts it like this:

> The church is the crucible that makes us disciples, the furnace that burns away selfishness and self-preference and every notion of a life of self-fulfillment and forges a purity of faith that is an affront to a world intoxicated with the self... And sometimes the only way we can let it make us disciples is to stay when we want to bolt... If you are not being inconvenienced regularly in church you are probably doing it wrong.[23]

There may be a time when it is the right thing to do to move from one church community to another – for example, if your church has deviated significantly on a core theological issue. But it is important to ask ourselves when we think about moving if we are doing so in the spirit of a disciple or of a consumer. Our wayward hearts and our culture would tip us towards the latter.

And there is never a good time to disconnect altogether. If you are reading this and you have stopped going to church and being part of a local family of God, our deep encouragement to you is to return, for your benefit and for that of others. If you

---

23 Grothe, *The Power of Place*, p. 179.

have believing friends or family who have got out of the habit of gathering with other Christians, encourage them to come home. If people find Sundays difficult because of work patterns or other commitments (your authors fit into this category), is there a regular midweek group they can belong to? I, Phil, was speaking at a conference a couple of years after the pandemic and on a morning run got chatting to one of the guests. I asked him what the Lord was doing in his life that week. 'I stopped going to church when lockdown started', he said, 'but I think as a result of this week I will go back.' We are convinced there are hundreds of thousands of believers in the UK who are not part of a local church, and we are poorer for it.

It's not about you

The 'you do you' drumbeat resonating through every Instagram reel and advertising campaign means that we can often make decisions based solely on the premise of 'What's in it for me?' When it comes to church, the answer to 'What's in it for us?' is the fact that church is vital in our ongoing formation into a disciple of Jesus. As the popular modern writer on spirituality John Mark Comer emphatically states, 'You can't follow Jesus alone. Not shouldn't, can't.'[24]

But growing as a disciple is only one benefit of being connected in mutually life-giving community. Disciples lay down their lives for their friends and, as such, ask the question, 'What's in it for others?' When we show up at church gatherings, we bring something into that physical space that no one else can. When we are not there, the room is impoverished as a result. Before you decide to stay at home on a Sunday, remember the gift that you are to your community and what you bring just by being there. Most importantly, the

24 J. M. Comer, *Practicing the Way: Be with Jesus. Become like him. Do as he did* (London: Form, 2024), p. 108.

people of God together, and your part among them, glorifies Jesus. Ephesians 3:21 says, 'to him be glory in the church and in Christ Jesus throughout all generations'. As the Church we reflect the glory of God; when we gather together, he is not just there with us (Matthew 18:20), but we lift his name high.

Church can be difficult. Mainly because it is made up of broken, imperfect and sinful people. As the great Victorian Baptist pastor Charles Spurgeon (who brilliantly modelled so many of the postures of good news people we have been exploring in this book) said:

> If I had never joined a church till I had found one that was perfect, I should never have joined one at all; and the moment I did join it, if I had found one, I should have spoiled it, for it would not have been a perfect church after I had become a member of it.[25]

Occasionally, the teaching will be too long, too short, too challenging, not inspirational or not practical enough. Sometimes the songs will be too high, too low, too modern, too old-fashioned, too loud or too contemplative. Disagreements over things such as candlesticks, carpets, sound systems and seating arrangements can turn into lifelong feuds. Leaders will fall. Friends will let us down badly. But being part of a community really matters. It is the lifeblood of discipleship. Spurgeon finished by saying, 'Still, imperfect as it is, it is the dearest place on earth to us.'[26] It's why the author to the Hebrews urges us, 'let us consider how we may spur one another on toward love and good deeds, not giving up meeting together, as some are in the habit of doing, but encouraging one another – and all the more as you see the Day approaching' (Hebrews 10:24–25).

---

25 'Spurgeon Quotes', PrinceofPreachers.org, https://www.princeofpreachers.org/quotes/the-dearest-place-on-earth-to-us (accessed 23 October 2024).

26 'Spurgeon Quotes'.

Disciples are the goal

We love seeing decisions for Jesus but making lifelong disciples must be the aim for all of us. We are both captivated by the way that Jesus did this. When he wanted to change the world the first thing he did was start a youth group. Jesus was in his early thirties and the disciples were mainly teenagers.[27] Jesus did 'life on life' with this small bunch of young people and poured everything he had into them. His call on their life was a challenging one as he beckoned them to leave all they had and follow him. Once they were with him, he then empowered them profoundly. We love the moment at the feeding of the 5,000 in John 6 when Jesus turns to his youth group and asks who has any lunch for the huge crowd assembled. Eleven of the disciples do nothing but Andrew brings a boy's packed lunch to Jesus and he feeds the field with twelve basketfuls left over. What a moment for Andrew to realise his part in the kingdom. Jesus always wants the disciples involved.

Jesus also teaches them the values that really matter. In John 13, they are sitting around wanting dinner after a hard day but can't eat as their feet have not been washed. This was slaves' work and a particularly humble task – to such an extent that even a Jewish slave would not be required to wash feet. The only rank of person deemed low enough to do this work was a Gentile slave. They are all looking at one another wondering what to do, when Jesus gets a bucket and a towel and reverses the economy of the world by washing their feet. Here, the Saviour of the world becomes the Servant King as he shows that humility, mercy and love are the most important things.

He continues to teach them so much and in John 21 we see the reality of genuine forgiveness as Peter is restored on the beach. I, Gavin, have stood on that beach in Galilee and it is incredibly

---

27 G. Calver and S. Whiting, *Lazy, Anti-Social & Selfish?* (Oxford: Monarch Books, 2009), p. 14.

moving to realise that Jesus showed Peter that failure is never final with God. He is the God of the second chance and we too must be quick to forgive those around us. Finally, in Matthew 28, Jesus teaches his youth group the importance of reaching out and all playing our part in the Great Commission.

There is so much more we could write. It's a fun after-dinner question to debate exactly when the disciples themselves became Christians. We can make a journey to faith so linear and yet Jesus shows us that much of our discipleship can begin even before we surrender our lives to him. We are so challenged by the Jesus model and wonder if we need to entirely reconsider some of what we are doing in the light of this example. The American pastor Rich Villodas put it this way on his Twitter/X account:

If Jesus spent 8 hrs a day, every day, for 3 years w/his disciples, he would have spent over 8,000 hours w/them. And after all that time, they still had major gaps. 1 hour a week on Sunday will never change people. We need a life that abides in him, with the support of others.[28]

Perhaps it is time for our models of discipleship to return to being far more life-on-life driven as opposed to programme orientated.

Back to basics...

We are both at a stage of life now that can only be described as middle-aged. However we choose to fight this, there is no changing the fact that we are no longer young. What this also highlights is how different things were in our early years of discipleship to some of what happens now. We grew up learning memory verses all the time, in a culture where Christianity was far more warmly

28 R. Villodas [@richvillodas], 'If Jesus spent 8 hours a day' [Tweet], X, 2 January 2023, https://x.com/richvillodas/status/1609908118430916608 (accessed 23 October 2024).

welcomed and embraced, and at a time when the Christian story was far more widely known. This was then enhanced through the children's work of the likes of Ishmael who so helpfully furthered our theological knowledge through his incredible work with the Glorie Company. It was on a recent Calver holiday that Gavin introduced his teenagers to a number of Ishmael Bible songs and we've all found ourselves humming along and singing them since.

I, Phil, have had the wonderful joy of seeing a friend from university come to faith in the last few months, having lived far from God for most of his life. He also lives over 100 miles away so we don't see each other that often, but he is really keen to let his embryonic faith grow. So, every Friday morning at 6:15 a.m., we jump on Zoom, study the Bible and pray. It has reminded me of the power of two disciples of Jesus keeping it simple and seeking growth in Jesus together. For both of us, it has been transformative.

Things may be more secular and challenging now but that is no reason for us to not keep doing the right things. Holiness may seem out of fashion but it is so profoundly important that we as good news people are distinct from the culture. Instead of working out how much we can get away with, this feels like a time to relentlessly pursue Jesus and rediscover what it looks like to be set apart for him. Equally, spiritual disciplines such as prayer, Bible reading, fasting and keeping the Sabbath do not seem the most exciting things to some but they are utterly fundamental to our personal and corporate discipleship and to growing in Jesus.

As secular culture has continued to impact the nation, we at the Evangelical Alliance have introduced an ethos and practice statement for our team.[29] Fundamentally, it is a basics of Christian discipleship that we get each of the team to ascribe to annually. We are not sure this would have been needed when we were younger but it feels

---

29 'Ethos and Practice of the Evangelical Alliance', Evangelical Alliance, 28 February 2023, https://www.eauk.org/assets/files/downloads/Evangelical-Alliance-Ethos-Practice.pdf (accessed 23 October 2024).

like we need to continue to do all we can to fight the secularisation of the Church and stand firm as disciples in our cultural day. To unpack that, let's consider an inspirational example from a totally different context. Iran has the fastest-growing church in the world.[30] When the pressure really kicked in there, it was said that many of the 'converts' fled but the disciples remained.[31] We are in a totally different landscape but as the pressure rises in the years ahead in the UK, we hope and pray that we will all have the foundations and discipleship base to be able to withstand the cultural pressure to confirm to the secular landscape instead of the kingdom of heaven.

When decisions become disciples

At a church not long ago, a lady approached me, Gavin, after the service to thank me for my ministry. I naively assumed that she was speaking about my preaching that morning. I said that it had been a real pleasure to be with them and a delight to speak. She swiftly interrupted me and said, 'Oh no, I'm not thanking you for today's talk. That was really average. I'm thanking you for over ten years ago when you went into a particular young offenders' institute to preach and my son, who was an inmate at the time, surrendered his life to Jesus.' She continued, 'What's amazing is that the same son is now going into that same young offenders' institute as part of the chaplaincy team to help other young men encounter Jesus for themselves too.' I was absolutely blown away. Over the years, I had learned to accept that the impact I saw in young offenders' institutions was arguably not entirely accurate. This young man

---

30 S. Eekhoff Zylstra, 'Meet the World's Fastest-growing Evangelical Movement', The Gospel Coalition, 8 February 2021, https://www.thegospelcoalition.org/article/meet-the-worlds-fastest-growing-evangelical-movement/ (accessed 23 October 2024).

31 For amazing testimony of what this looks like in Iran, and how it relates to Jesus' teaching on discipleship, see Phil Moore's *The Forgotten Manifesto of Jesus: How revival in Iran is spreading across the world* (London: IVP, 2024) for inspiration and practical help.

was one of the hands in the air, perhaps to gain some additional time out of his cell. But somewhere further down the line, that decision became a disciple with rhythms and habits that reflect his apprenticeship to Jesus. Across the UK, we see many churches that are getting this balance right and we see it as a key tension to hold for us in this season.

Taking it further

- Look back at the ways in which people are coming to faith. When you think about your own friends and neighbours, which ways might help them move forward on their journey of faith? How might these impact your social media use? How might your prayer life and friendships be affected as you consider your calling as a good news disciple maker?
- Where do you see the effect of individualism on your relationship with God and others? How might the Lord be inviting you to greater interdependence and to play your part in the body of believers? How might we combat the impact of consumerism on our faith?
- Get a copy of the *Finding Jesus* report. Celebrate the insights from almost 300 new adult Christians and hear some of their stories.[32] What do you find surprising and what resonates with your experience? Take some time to pray for your friends who are not yet Christians and commit to intensifying your prayers for them.

Recommended reading

Story Bearer: How to share your faith with your friends by Phil Knox (London: IVP, 2020) – We can all grow in our heart and ability to

---

32 *Finding Jesus* (2025).

share our faith with our friends. In *Story Bearer*, Phil explains that evangelism can be highly relational and is based on great story telling. This book is intended to help all of us become confident and natural good news bearers to our friends, neighbours, colleagues and family members.

Revival Ready: Rethinking kingdom, discipleship and Church by Steve and Esther Uppal (Wolverhampton: All Nations Publishing, 2022) – This book looks at what is needed in the days ahead and explores the practical implications of this for individuals, families and churches. It is really helpful in enabling us to rethink things in our day in order to shape a brighter future.

The themes of this chapter can be explored further using small group resources, videos and discussion questions. Delve deeper at www.goodnewspeople.church

8

We need to be united and diverse

Be united with other Christians. A wall with loose bricks is not good. The bricks must be cemented together.
Corrie Ten Boom[1]

I, Gavin, arrived at the conference in good time. There was already a real sense of excitement and anticipation in the building. The crowd was growing and we were all enjoying tucking into all kinds of South American delicacies. I was taken off to a side room and the evening ahead was explained to me through translation. We would be worshipping, praying and contending for a new move of God. I was asked to preach for an hour and then minister off the back of that. I spoke with my Spanish translator and explained to her some of the stories and content I would be sharing in the evening ahead.

We entered the auditorium. It was absolutely packed full of people hungry to worship, intercede for the nations and hear the Word of God. I was nervously excited to be getting up to speak and prayed a simple prayer to ask the Lord to calm my nerves and give me peace. I did my best to join in with and follow the dynamic worship, despite it all being in Spanish. I was profoundly grateful to the lady sitting with me translating as much as she could, while the pastor spoke powerfully. The atmosphere was electric, the people expectant and the sense of the presence of God as palpable as I have

---

1 'Quotes on Unity in Christ', Faith Unlocked, https://faithunlocked.wordpress. com/2014/08/02/quotes-on-unity-in-christ/ (accessed 19 December 2024).

known. I got up to speak and the translator joined me as I began to share a message around what revival could look like.

I'd seen scenes like the one I found myself in on social media from all over the world: loads of the people of God gathered together for a powerful time of prayer, worship, repentance and ministry. The difference this time was that this gathering was not taking place in another nation; I was ministering in London. It was a gathering for many of the Spanish-speaking congregations in the UK and it was an incredible occasion. My dear friend Pastor Carlos had invited me to share and it was another of those occasions on which I reflected on the great heterogeneity that makes up UK evangelicalism.

The posture we will explore in this chapter is that of celebrating this kind of diversity while also contending for unity. Our Church is made up of so many people from such different backgrounds, stories and contexts. We believe this kind of unity is theoretically simple, but costly and demanding in practice. It demands much of us but it is worth fighting for.

The Church

As a follower of Jesus, you are part of something amazing. In a fractured and divided world, it is easy to lose sight of the astonishing connection that we have, to what is so much bigger than ourselves. One evangelist tells this story to describe its scale and brilliance. He was sitting on a plane on the tarmac at Heathrow airport when the passenger next to him asked him the question, 'What do you do?' Reluctant to tell her he was a Reverend, his reply was as creative as it was provocative. He told her that he worked for a global enterprise, with outlets in nearly every country, with hospitals, hospices, homeless shelters and orphanages. He enthused that his organisation helped marriages, delivered feeding programmes, educational courses and justice and reconciliation initiatives. 'Basically' he summarised, 'we look after people from birth to death and we deal in the area of behavioural alteration.' The passenger's 'Wow!' was so loud that others turned to listen to the conversation. 'What's it called?' she enquired. 'It's called the Church,' came the evangelist's reply, 'Have you heard of it?'[2]

The Church of Jesus Christ is absolutely brilliant. And one of the great joys of our roles is that we get to see it in all its diversity. One of the main reasons for writing this book is to give evangelicals a flavour of the family and story that we are part of. We wish we could take you personally into the rooms and gatherings that we are invited into, to meet the extraordinary leaders and see the life bursting from communities of faith. When we compare notes and share the stories of our travels, one of the things that enthuses us most is the diverse range of what we experience.

A significant factor in the current health of UK evangelicalism is reverse mission. For many years, this nation sent missionaries all over the world but more recently we have been delighted to receive them. Our friend Pastor Agu Irukwu has been an incredible gift to the UK. He has been the senior pastor of Jesus House in Brent Cross for many years and was previously overseeing the whole of the Redeemed Christian Church of God which is the fastest growing denomination in the UK.[3] I, Gavin, will always remember the first time Pastor Agu had me to speak at a prayer meeting. I was used to such gatherings being a few folks in a cold room, drinking bad coffee and praying for about an hour. This occasion was somewhat different. It was called *Festival of Life* and there were 40,000 people gathered in the Excel arena to pray all night for revival in the UK.[4] I

2 See TBN, 'How to Explain What You Do, When You're a Pastor' [Video], YouTube, 13 November 2014, https://www.youtube.com/watch?v=L6TGxKvSqH8 for the full clip (accessed 23 October 2024).

3 G. Luke, 'The Inside Story of the UK's Fastest Growing Church', Premier Christianity, 30 October 2024, https://www.premierchristianity.com/uk-church/the-inside-story-of-the-uks-fastest-growing-church/18429.article (accessed 11 November 2024).

4 Festival of Life, https://www.festivaloflife.org.uk (accessed 11 November 2024).

was one of just a handful of white faces and was blown away by the privilege of ministering in that space. As I travelled home from the arena in the early hours of the morning, I found myself thanking the Lord for the incredible impact that majority world evangelicals are having in the UK.

Some churches have been part of their community for hundreds of years, the stone walls soaked with the prayers of centuries of saints, and yet have moved with the times. When you take a twenty-first-century snapshot, there is as much life as ever before. Others are embryonic church plants, pioneered by modern-day apostles, bursting with the innovative energies of a business start-up. Still others are demonstrations that things that are dying can be revitalised. Buildings where worshippers gathered for decades that had been sold to become carpet warehouses or nightclubs have been repurchased and repurposed by the family of God and are now home to believers once more.

Some Sunday mornings require a greater cultural adaptation than others. We are both white and middle-aged. Occasionally, we are very much the ethnic minority in the room. We have to be quick to get over any inhibitions and celebrate the vibrancy and spiritual life as these far exceed our awkward attempts at dancing! In other settings, we might be translated into Punjabi, Romanian, Korean or Portuguese. This means that a forty-five-minute sermon can last an hour and half!

The UK Church also crosses every socio-economic boundary. Sometimes, the postcodes we type into our satnavs are some of the most sought-after in worldly terms. On other occasions, we head to some of the poorest and most forgotten neighbourhoods. We both live within 100 yards of evangelical Anglican churches in parishes at vastly different ends of the economic spectrum – one in the top 2% of deprivation, the other in the bottom 10%. Yet both are made up of all ages and stages and are thriving in our communities. We have worshipped in rooms standing next to millionaires on one side and those with next to nothing in earthly terms on the other.

There is also diversity in the ages represented in some expressions. In some church families, the majority present are grandparents, crowned with the wisdom that only years of experience can bring, heroes of the faith whose journeys ooze stories of God's faithfulness and grace. In those congregations, we bring the average age down by a few years. In others, we feel elderly. There are loads of examples of churches exploding with radical followers of Jesus almost exclusively from Gen Z. *The Times* reports that Gen Z are only half as likely as their parents to identify as atheists.[5] Reports of the Church struggling among young adults in many places have been drastically overstated and what we see is a full variety of age groups reflected in UK evangelicalism.

That's what makes you beautiful

There are few sights more captivating than a bride on her wedding day. When the words 'Please stand for the bride' are uttered, no one chooses that moment to check their phone or begins to admire the architecture of the church building. No one is reaching for their order of service, curious about which hymns have been chosen by the couple. As the doors open and she takes her slow steps down the aisle, all eyes are on her. It is a breathtaking moment.

This is the image God uses to describe the Church.

Don't miss this. Church often gets a rough time. When you type the words, 'Why is church so...' into Google, it predicts the next word for you. After 'important', the next few suggestions are things like 'long', 'early', 'hard' and 'boring'. And the negativity can come just as much from friendly fire as external criticism. We can be

---

5   K. Burgess, 'Gen Z Half as Likely as Their Parents to Identify as Atheists', https://www.thetimes.com/uk/religion/article/gen-z-half-as-likely-as-their-parents-to-identify-as-atheists-wp2vl0l29 (accessed 27 March 2025).

extremely hard on ourselves. This is why the biblical image of the bride is so important. Beauty, they say, is in the eye of the beholder. And in this instance, the beholder is the living God, the Creator of heaven and earth. And he says that the Church is beautiful.

But what is it that makes us look so good? As John looks forward to the future of the people of God, he sees the twenty-four elders and four living creatures describing those purchased for God as being, 'persons from every tribe and language and people and nation' (Revelation 5:9). This description of diversity comes before the idea of God's people being his bride (Revelation 19:7). There seems to be an intrinsic connectedness between this bride's beauty and her diversity. While we are waiting in anticipation for the marriage and the glorious banquet John's writings are looking forward to, this connection invites us to marvel and wonder at how God calls such different people together to be united to him.

The differences across age, race, background and story we have described are partly responsible for what makes the Church so beautiful. We had better get used to them. They are a picture of heaven.

When diversity leads to division

We naturally gravitate towards people with whom we share things in common. When we enter a room full of strangers, we are instinctively far more likely to make or grow connections with people who look like us, think, vote, speak and laugh like us. Christians of a feather flock together. But this also means in our fallen nature, that we can be suspicious and slow to trust people who are not like us. There is nothing wrong with naturally forming relationship with those who we share commonalities with, but it harms the body of Christ when divisions develop and when we fail to make relationships with those who are different. And this is not a new issue.

Although there was some diversity among the twelve apostles, they were largely a monocultural group of men from the same religious background, geographical context and age group.[6] But on the day of Pentecost, as the fuse is lit on the explosion of church life, 'every nation under heaven' is invited to join the party (Acts 2:5). Luke describes the variety of those present,

> Parthians, Medes and Elamites; residents of Mesopotamia, Judea and Cappadocia, Pontus and Asia, Phrygia and Pamphylia, Egypt and the parts of Libya near Cyrene; visitors from Rome (both Jews and converts to Judaism); Cretans and Arabs.
> (Acts 2:9)

Of the 3,000 added to the embryonic church, we can assume some came from these backgrounds. A diverse Church was always the plan. It is as old as the Great Commission.

And yet when things grow rapidly in size, they also often grow in complexity. Those initial 3,000 have become billions. It is impossible to know how many churches there are globally, but a quick Google search tells you that the billions of Christians on planet Earth are part of around 37 million churches, which fit into a mind-boggling 34,000 denominations.[7] And Jesus anticipates the potential divisions this growth would cause. It is as if he knew what would happen to his Church. Before his 'body on earth' was even unveiled, its founder's prayer is not for growth, strategic thinking or innovation. Jesus' prayer is that those who believe in him would be one. We will now turn to why the unity matters. It is simply that it is at the heart of God. It is what Jesus prays for in John 17.

---

6 See Knox, *The Best of Friends*, Chapter 6, for a breakdown of the similarities and differences between the twelve disciples.

7 'How Many Churches Are There in the World?', Quora, https://www.quora.com/How-many-churches-are-there-in-the-world (accessed 23 October 2024).

Jesus' prayer comes in what is one of the most impactful and profound chapters in the whole of Scripture. Canadian theologian Don Carson emphasised, 'What is unique about this prayer rests neither on form nor on literary associations but on him who offers it and when.'[8] The Son of God is hours away from execution and resurrection, and his heart is set on the future unity of the global enterprise to come.

Unity

My prayer is not for them alone. I pray also for those who will believe in me through their message, that all of them may be one, Father, just as you are in me and I am in you. May they also be in us so that the world may believe that you have sent me. I have given them the glory that you gave me, that they may be one as we are one – I in them and you in me – so that they may be brought to complete unity. Then the world will know that you sent me and have loved them even as you have loved me.
(John 17:20–23)

'That all of them may be one'

In a world of brokenness, pain, confusion, division and lack of trust, there are few things more important than the call for the Church to unite as one at this moment in our gospel mission to the world. This cry for Christian unity seems to be getting louder, perhaps because many of the divisions in society are growing wider. In our culture separation, hostility and isolation are seemingly rampant – mentally, physically, tribally, spiritually, geographically and emotionally – and yet the Lord calls his children to cross all of these divides by coming together and reflecting his glory. Surely in

8 D. A. Carson, *The Gospel According to John* (Leicester: Apollos, 1994), p. 551.

a world that is torn apart, the reality of a united body becomes even more appealing to those who are lost?

For the Evangelical Alliance, Jesus' prayer for unity in John 17 has always been a central passage that we long to see lived out through our ministry. It was this passage that was quoted by the Presbyterian David King at the gathering of leaders in Liverpool in 1845. Here, Jesus prays passionately that the Church may be united, that all of them may be one (verse 21) and that they may be brought to complete unity (verse 23). It is incredible to think that, as Pastor Malcolm Duncan points out, 'In one of the most difficult moments of His entire ministry, with the cross looming before Him and guards on the way to arrest Him, He asked His Father that we would be one.'[9] That is the importance of this unity and we must do all we can to be united in our day. Jesus longs that people from every tribe, tongue and nation would be one because it will point the world to the love and salvation available to them in Christ. Unity is not an option. It is something that is on God's heart for his children, so we can be certain he will aid us in seeking it.

'As we are one'

In John 17, Jesus prays for unity; a harmony of spirit, mind, heart and will. It is not some form of enforced conformity but rather an expression of unity in difference. Just as in the Trinity there are differing functions, so too within the body there will be a beautiful variety of gifts and service. The global family of God is the most wonderful picture of different ages, races, attitudes, characteristics, gifts and hopes all brought to God to serve together and glorify him. Jesus is praying that God would do it, not us. It is not possible for us to create this kind of unity for ourselves. It cannot be forced and no amount of human effort can make it happen. Clearly, such unity is a work of God. However, we can play

9 M. Duncan, *One for All: The foundations* (Oxford: Monarch Books, 2017), p. 84.

our part in expressing this unity and doing all we possibly can to maintain it.

'Then the world will know'

As we read some of those words of Jesus again in John 17 – 'so that the world may believe that you have sent me' (verses 21, 23) – we are reminded why we are united too. It is not for our own sakes but to point people to Jesus. This unity should be so noticeable, observable and tangible that those outside of the Church notice it and are drawn towards it. Anyone who sees a united Church will be profoundly impacted by it. John Stott puts it this way:

> This unity will make a definite impact on the world. Just as Jesus disclosed the unseen God to the world by becoming flesh (John 1:14), so the Church will be a visible revelation of the unseen Father and his love.[10]

It is profoundly clear then that the ultimate aim of such unity is not for Christians to simply enjoy it – but for the world to notice it and, as a result, come to believe that the Father has sent the Son.[11] Tom Wright writes:

> The world will see, and know, that this kind of human community, united across all traditional barriers of race, custom, gender or class, can only come from the action of the creator God. 'So that the world may believe...'[12]

This unity must be outward facing. Little convinces the world more of the gospel than the countercultural unity of the Church. No other community, group or tribe can unite so profoundly across

10 J. Stott, *The Message of John* (Leicester: IVP, 1993), p. 248.

11 M. Duncan, *One for All: The implications* (Oxford: Monarch Books, 2017), p. 76.

12 T. Wright, *John for Everyone* (London: SPCK, 2002), p. 99.

human divides as we seek to be the family of God. This is not just about sitting around in cosy huddles being nice to one another, this unity is part of the Great Commission: to go into the world and make disciples. We go out together, in relationship; we do not go alone. We all long for people from every tribe, nation and tongue to encounter Christ, so let's unite around reaching them with the gospel. Yes, witnessing can often feel like a fruitless task and one that is so hard to do. But if we are engaged in it together, we embody Christ's oneness and demonstrate a powerful message to a divided world. Imagine what we could we do for the kingdom in mission together, all playing our part, cheering one another on and doing it alongside each other.

In the end, Jesus' powerful prayer in John 17 leaves us with a clear and profound challenge. He cries out to his Father, longing for a unity among all his followers that will be so visible and powerful that it will lead to an openness and receptivity to the gospel message of the Church from the world around it. Theologian Phil Moore sums it up this way, 'divided we fall, but together we can march as a united force to reach the world, and to succeed as one for the Father's glory.'[13]

Unity as evangelicals

But what does unity look like specifically for evangelicals? In Chapters 1 and 2 we identified the characteristics that hold us together. The primary distinctive was that good news people place a particular emphasis on the Bible as the primary source of authority when it comes to determining theological truth. This infers that there are other followers of Jesus who do not do this and lean equally – or place different emphases – on Scripture, tradition, experience and reason. It is an important question to ask what

---

13 P. Moore, *Straight to the Heart of John* (Oxford: Monarch Books, 2012), p. 224.

unity looks like with our brothers and sisters with whom we agree on many things, but do not see eye-to-eye on matters of primary importance. We want to suggest that this means that there are a couple of distinct levels of unity that we can engage with.

At the first level, we need a unity across all believers who confess Jesus as Lord. There is no 'evangelical' section in heaven: we will share eternity with fellow Christians with whom we disagree theologically on some significant issues. Christian unity is an area that evangelicals have not always been that keen on or effective at, but it is important. In our advocacy work, there are often issues that we can take to government with a breadth of Christian unity that makes the impact even greater. Gavin will often find himself in the corridors of power alongside Christian leaders of other traditions seeking to bring a united voice on shared concerns.

But there is another level of unity that we can go to with fellow evangelicals. Where there is agreement on the supreme authority of the Bible, the uniqueness of Jesus, the significance of the cross, the need for conversion and the desire to make a difference, there is an even greater synergy. It means that, for example, we can engage together in evangelistic initiatives – because there is a common enough understanding of what the gospel is, how we are inviting people to respond and a longing for conversion in the first place. This is the kind of unity that inspired the pioneers of the Evangelical Alliance and is embodied by the hundreds of expressions of evangelical unity across the UK today. As we explained in Chapter 3, we are a stream of over eighty networks, denominations or streams within the Evangelical Alliance membership. It is a joy to be part of this and we are so excited about the days ahead.

Strength in diversity

Every context in which we find ourselves is different and has its own way of doing things, its own leaders operating in their own style.

People often tell us that they are not a typical Evangelical Alliance-type church. In truth, nowhere is! There is such diversity within UK evangelicalism. When heading off to speak, our wives will often ask when we will be back. At many churches we know, the service will definitely be no longer than an hour and fifteen minutes, so we can give an almost to-the-minute time as to when we'll be home. In others, we simply have to say that we hope we will be back that day!

Theologically, we are both quite charismatic, and very free and physically expressive in worship. However, in many places we visit, this is not the way that they encounter the Lord and we respect that fully. Although it often isn't the style we are used to, we love the variety we encounter. We honour the way that some people put a huge emphasis on the teaching of the Bible, whereas for others the time of sung worship is the key element of any gathering. In some contexts, people hold hospitality as central to all they do; in other settings, community engagement is fundamental. All of these matter so much and we love the variety of the Evangelical Church in all its diversity. There is so much for us to all learn from one another. We find this exciting and something to really celebrate. The basis of faith that holds the Evangelical Alliance together allows for different views on all kinds of secondary issues. This can create a real challenge but also a profound opportunity to go forward as one. We really believe this is the kind of unity Jesus prayed for in John 17 when he longed that we would be so united that the world would notice and be drawn to himself.

After all, life would be incredibly dull if we were all the same. It is a real joy encountering the differences we have while also holding to the main thing and keeping that central. One of our longings moving forward would be that the Evangelical Alliance will continue to be able to represent and serve all evangelicals in the UK and celebrate our differences while also rejoicing in the fact that on the key issues we stand shoulder to shoulder, we move forward as one and we make Jesus known together.

How we build unity

One of the core emphases of the work of the Evangelical Alliance has always been to provide the table around which the leaders from the church in a city or town can get together and unite. These conversations have led to an understanding of the journey by which unity happens. What we will describe here – in part, thanks to the work of Augland, Boschker et al. – are five Cs that form the layers through which leaders often pass as unity deepens in a place.[14] These ideas are mostly for leaders, but we can all play a part in praying for and encouraging this journey to take place.

1 Competition and comparison

At our worst, our mindset towards other likeminded churches in our area is like that of a business owner moving onto new turf. Other churches are not co-labourers in the harvest field, but competitors for the crops. We are not so much on the same team but jockeying for league position. This in turn leads to a spirit of comparison. The UK Church is full of extraordinarily gifted people. One of the challenges of serving on the same team as others who excel in their field is that we can begin to compare ourselves with them. We can identify with King Saul when he heard the refrain, 'Saul has slain in his thousands, and David in his tens of thousands' (1 Samuel 18:7). In response, we read he was 'very angry' (verse 8). Our mindset must be that we compete together for the kingdom of God, rather than against one another. Otherwise, comparison will end up clouding the clarity of our calling.[15]

14 O. Augland et al., *Together: Equip to multiply* (Berlin: Exponential, 2021).

15 R. Madu [@robertmadu], 'Comparing will consistently cloud the clarity of your call!' [Tweet], X, 17 July 2023, https://twitter.com/robertmadu/status/357294607324815361 (accessed 23 October 2024).

2 Coexistence

When we stop competing, the next level of unity is coexistence. Here, we have moved on from hostility, but there is no depth of relationship. In workplace terms, the leaders of other churches are the people you smile at as you pass in the corridor but you are meeting on the plateau of platitudes.

3 Communication

When we begin to become more intentional about our relational unity we begin to communicate. While there may be differences in style and approach, we discover that we are standing on the same common foundations. We identify mutual struggles and celebrate one another's successes.

4 Cooperation

Cooperation is the shift from knowing one another to helping one another. Resources, time and ideas are shared. I, Phil, once spoke at a church weekend away where another church brought a team of volunteers to do all the cooking, cleaning, childcare and hospitality. The next weekend, the arrangement swapped over: the church that had been blessed became the blessing to those who had served. All this took place on the same site and the two churches shared the burden, cost and infrastructure. This is cooperation.

5 Collaboration

At this stage, church leaders and communities dream together and share a common vision for the transformation of their place. There is such a profound sense of unity that Christians in a town or city begin to talk of the one 'church' in that place that meet in different buildings, not many 'churches' that don't know one another. When a crisis arises, the Church can respond as one. Collaborating leaders will plan together and engage in events and initiatives that have deeper impact because they are greater than the sum of their parts. When the Church collaborates, members share one another's battles and blessings and genuinely want the best for the collective whole, regardless of which congregation grows.

Progressing through the layers

We see churches across the UK at every level of these five Cs, but we are encouraged that the Church is becoming more and more connected in our day. What can we do to help us move from competing to collaborating?

Common prayer

There are few things that build cohesion and bonds of trust like prayer. While there are many practices that we may disagree on, we are yet to meet a Christian who thinks we should not pray. And there is something that happens when we pray and worship Jesus together that strengthens the cords of unity between us. This was one of the core activities of the early church that contributed to their rapid growth. Moreover, it was distinctively revolutionary when compared to other religious groups in the first and second centuries. Christians prayed together. Pagans did not.[16]

And when we speak to leaders who have been on the journey through the five layers of unity, prayer together is the single most important common theme. This kind of regular prayer can breathe life and resilience into desperate situations. I, Phil, recently met a retired vicar who had ministered for decades in a tough parish where crime was rife and the needs of the community were overwhelming. In his early days, this minister turned up to a meeting with other leaders in the town. As they each suggested that they shared their encouragements from recent weeks, his discouraged eyes could only look at the floor. When their attentions turned to ask him

---

16 A. Kreider, *The Patient Ferment of the Early Church: The improbable rise of Christianity in the Roman Empire* (Grand Rapids: Baker Academic, 2016), p. 205.

how he was getting on, his monosyllabic, honest reply was one you don't often hear in church. As a result of this vulnerable moment, the other leaders suggested they come to his house each week to pray together. This gathering went on to last for many years and was catalytic in this vicar faithfully staying the course in that community and led to lifelong transformative friendships.

Friendship

Christians should be the best friends in the world. We have the relational God who lives within us by his Spirit. Jesus said that people would know that we are his disciples because we love one another (John 13:35). When we eat, talk and drink coffee together, we reflect the relational beauty of the Acts church who 'had everything in common... Every day they continued to meet together... and ate together' (Acts 2:44–46). In a world drowning in loneliness and division, as we prioritise becoming better friends – especially with those who are different from us – more and more we become the answer to Jesus' prayer that we might be one.

For leaders this is a particularly significant issue. Leadership can be really lonely. Dan Allender soberly states:

> The data are fairly clear about those at the top of the organisational chart. The higher you are, the more rarified are your friendships. The ones that last over countless crises and conflicts are forged in iron. And those friendships, like true soul mates, are as rare as oxygen at 30,000 feet. Therefore, one price of formal leadership is being alone.[17]

In the battles and blessings of church life, friendship for leaders within churches provide valuable camaraderie, but real friendships with leaders across a town or city also give priceless perspective and

17 D. Allender, *Leading with a Limp: Take full advantage of your most powerful weakness* (New York: Waterbrook, 2006), p. 33.

support from outside the immediate church community. They also provide the platform for genuine cooperation and collaboration. Ministry should be fun at times and is best enjoyed with friends. If you want to know how you can support your leaders, friendship may be the greatest gift you can give.

Clarity

To reach the stage of collaboration, honest conversations are needed about a shared theological vision. Leaders especially need to know the common ground on which they stand and what secondary issues can be put to one side. Above all, a mutual understanding of the core components of the gospel are essential. We do not have to agree on everything and healthy diversity on some issues can be a strength rather than a weakness. We are regularly in rooms with those from most major denominations, members of independent churches, reformed and charismatic, old and new expressions. All of them can not only be friends but can also work together with a common denominator – a shared gospel heart and theology, a shared compelling vision for their town or city, and a shared longing for the lost. But to progress through the layers, we must be clear with one another on where we stand on the essentials.

When it works

When you see this kind of unity in action across an entire community, it can be breathtaking. In every town, village, city and hamlet within the UK, there are church leaders meeting, praying, dreaming and planning about what can be done together for the benefit of their place.

One of the things we do at the Evangelical Alliance is regularly go on mini-tours to six different locations over three days. The aim is to meet with as many local church leaders as possible over food.

To hear what is going on, learn lessons from the ground and make sure what we are doing nationally reflects what is needed locally. On one such gathering, we were in Taunton for a breakfast and the unity was amazing. So many churches were coming together for the sake of the gospel. They were truly loving each other, preferring one another and putting the Lord's agenda at number one.

About eighteen months later I, Gavin, returned to Taunton to speak at their town-wide celebration. The leisure centre is the largest venue in town so that was booked and it was absolutely packed. Stories were shared of how the church was responding together to local needs, testimonies of salvation were everywhere and, as we worshipped as one church, the sense of unity was palpable. As I got up to speak it was an utter joy and a rare experience of something tangibly like the kind of unity Jesus prayed for in John 17.

Afterwards, the queue of people wanting to join the Evangelical Alliance was snaking around the venue and this was followed by a lunch with eleven of the local leaders. Seeing these folks fellowshipping together was wonderful and, despite them each having their own church to lead, they were genuinely more interested in the health of the whole church in Taunton as opposed to their own particular congregation. A couple of hours with these leaders flew by and I eventually drove home with a very full heart. We long to see this kind of unity throughout the UK.

In Teesside recently, over sixty churches united around evangelism. With a shared heart and strategy to reach people across their region. Together and as one, they sent thousands of people out on the streets to do social action projects to bless and serve their communities. They then gathered thousands more for a festival in a park where the gospel was proclaimed. This was word and deed mission together. But then, beautifully, because the relationships were already in place, the churches planned fifty Alpha courses across the towns and villages so that suitable follow-up could be run for those who responded. It is this kind of unity and togetherness that brings joy to the heart of God and enables us to do far more with others than we could on our own.

Gavin was recently up in Scotland at a prayer gathering of Christian leaders from across just about all the streams of evangelicalism. The unity in the room was incredible as around 300 church leaders gathered to pray from 7–10 p.m. and then the next day too from 7–10 a.m. These leaders represented a great breadth of the Scottish church and came together with no agenda other than to pray and fast for Scotland and to contend as one for a fresh move of God in the nation. With nothing else on the table, it was profoundly significant to be amongst this great crowd as we dreamt, wept and petitioned together for Scotland.

These three cases we mention are far from being isolated. We've been in united prayer meetings in Cardiff, town-wide celebrations in Rugby, joint youth events in Enniskillen, community outreach events in Newquay. Throughout the UK there is a growing unity around the desire to serve together, pray together, speak up together and, even more so, be one in order that more people would come to know Jesus.

Unity that changes the world

Over the last 100 years in particular, we have become more divided as a world. In his book *Fractured*, Jon Yates argues that sociologically there are always two opposing forces at work. The first is 'people like me syndrome' where, as we described, individuals gravitate towards others who look, think, laugh and vote like them. The second is the 'common life' where the natural circumstances of life bring people of different backgrounds, incomes and worldviews together. Yates's observation is that, in the last century, the dominant force has been 'people like me syndrome' which has meant that we are less and less likely to know people who are different from us.[18] Barriers have developed between young and old, rich and poor, black and white, right and left because they have been able to choose to avoid one another. We have filtered our friendships. As a result, we misunderstand, cancel, demonise and vilify people who are different from us simply because we do not know them.

The Church is, and must be, different. There is something so beautiful about the unity of the Church when it comes together as one and the world notices this profound togetherness. We do a lot around geographical unity. We seek to unite generationally too – but a strategic area for the Evangelical Alliance over the last decade or so has been that of unity across ethnicities. Our One People Commission has seen significant bridges built across previous ethnic boundaries.[19] This has been a wonderful thing to be involved in. We can show what it means to be brothers and sisters in Christ and to model a unity that the world finds very difficult to understand, let alone emulate.

I, Gavin, remember an occasion when my local church went for a men's curry night. It was at a local restaurant close to where I live and I know the guy who runs it fairly well. The gathering of men was twenty-two in number and ranged in age from a teenager to someone in their eighties. Across the group, there were fifteen different ethnicities and we were having a wonderful evening of fellowship together. My friend who ran the curry house asked, 'What on earth are you lot?'

'What do you think we are?' I replied.

'I think you are a church group.'

'Why is that?' I asked.

'Because you're a vicar type,' he observed.

---

18 J. Yates, *Fractured: How we learn to live together* (Manchester: Harper North, 2021), pp. 17–27.

19 'One People Commission', Evangelical Alliance, https://www.eauk.org/what-we-do/networks/one-people-commission (accessed 23 October 2024).

'What else would make you think we are a group from a church?'

'No other group in this community can get so diverse a bunch of people around a table enjoying a meal together.'

It was an incredible observation.

The strength of this kind of unity massively helps our advocacy work as we seek to speak up with one united voice within the corridors of power. The fact that we can represent such a diversity of people in the UK provides an even stronger platform for our voice to be heard, as we seek to speak up for Christian values, truth, hope and the evangelical population.

Healing for the nations

As we hear the words of Jesus' prayer for unity resounding through the ages, could it be answered in this moment? With the world at peak division, could the Church lead the way in modelling a unity so compelling and countercultural that it inspires renewal across fissured communities? Could it be that our love for one another, despite our differences, might lead the way to restoration between the factions in our broken society? And when dazzled and drawn by the irresistible brilliance of the people of God living in harmony, might this be catalytic in the revival of hearts we long to see: 'then the world will know' (John 13:35).

Revelation 22 reveals a vision of our united and restored future, with heaven full of every nation, tribe and tongue. At its centre is a tree. Notice that 'the leaves of the trees are for the healing of the nations' (Revelation 22:2). Gazing at this image, we are reminded of Jesus' description of himself as the vine and his invitation to us to remain connected to him as the branches (John 15:5–8). These words, spoken moments before his prayer for unity, must speak to us now as a Church. Abide in Jesus. Unite around him. And may our oneness in him and connection to the tree of life draw the lonely and fractured to know and love the Saviour of the world.

We are the Church
A city on a hill
The family of faith
A colony of hearts
A movement whose sum exceeds their parts

Spanning all generations, a gathering of the nations, from
    every vocation
African, Asian, Cockney, Scouse
In cathedral, school, cinema, house
Old to young, big to small
Anglican, Independent, Baptist, Pentecostal
Diverse in design, galvanised by the Gospel
From thousand-seater auditorium to plastic chairs in village hall
From Manchester to Mongolia to Maine to Montreal
From Sheffield to Strasbourg to Spain to Senegal
We are all for one, and one for all

And like tapestries woven, like a symphony of sound
It's in our diversity where our beauty is found

And yet
Divisions and divorces drive dangerous distractions
Pride and parochialism provoke painful partings
Friendly fire means walking wounded
Leaders limp
Tensions tear
But could we be the answer to our Saviour's prayer?

One
Like an orchestra in time, threads entwined

Dancers in cohesion, a regimented legion
And one, but we're not the same, we get to carry each other,
a kaleidoscope of colour
Knowing that unity is not uniformity
Commitment to Christ our central conformity
And might we do more united than is possible on our own?
Tirelessly together making Jesus known

So held by one grip, safe in one palm
Let's go all in for each other, for the gospel call
All for one and one for all
Good news people in a bad news world[20]

Taking it further

- A key component of unity is getting to know people who are different from you. Consider the spaces you find yourself in. Think about the opportunities where you have the choice to remain in your social comfort zone with those who are like you or cross the room and talk to others who are different. Challenge yourself to get to know a new person during coffee after church, over lunch at work, at the toddler group or social gathering.
- Read and meditate on John 17. Jesus clearly saw prayer as key to unity. He petitions the heavens for his followers to be one. Allow this example to shape your prayer life. Whatever your devotional rhythms look like, could you commit to regularly praying for unity in your local church, within your town, city or region and across the UK?

---

20 P. Knox, 'We Are the Church', 2024.

- We have discussed the importance of friendship in deepening unity. We have found that this subject is one that is much neglected by the Church. It is important to unity – but it also intersects with discipleship, evangelism, leadership and more. What could you do to turn up the volume of a conversation in church around the importance of friendship? How could you help people grow their relational muscles?

Recommended reading

Until Unity by Francis Chan (Colorado Springs: David C. Cook, 2021) – A call to believers and churches everywhere to do all we can to be more united. A passionate book arguing clearly for the fact that our unity as a Church must be more important to us all moving forward.

The Best of Friends: Choose wisely, care well by Phil Knox (London: IVP, 2023) – An exploration of the reasons behind the loneliness epidemic in our world and the astonishing power of friendship. A look at how Jesus built his circles of connections and an invitation to readers to discover how to grow their relational muscles.

The themes of this chapter can be explored further using small group resources, videos and discussion questions. Delve deeper at www.goodnewspeople.church

Conclusion

> My prayer is not for them alone. I pray also for those who will believe in me through their message, that all of them may be one, Father, just as you are in me and I am in you. May they also be in us so that the world may believe that you have sent me.
>
> John 17:20–21

I, Gavin, was sitting outside one of London's many pavement cafes with an old friend. It was a lovely summer's afternoon. We were catching up on family news and the fortunes of our football teams when my friend changed the tone of the conversation somewhat and said, 'I'm not an evangelical any more.' This was someone I had looked up to and sought theological insight from and so I was keen to know why he, of all people, had changed.

'I just don't agree with so many things… I struggle with God allowing His Son to die on a cross.' There was more. 'I think the Bible stories are a bit much and I don't relate to the God of them fully. And don't get me started on the narrow teaching around human sexuality.' I was a little stunned to say the least.

As the conversation continued, there was story after story of personal experiences that were framing my friend's theology far more than any theologian or indeed, Scripture, was. My overriding feeling was one of lament for a friend who was choosing a different type of Christianity to that which I understand. I listened intently for the rationale and reason behind all this change and, in the end, could not find it. My friend seemed to be basing so much of his thinking on his feelings, those of others around him and the overarching pressure from the culture.

'Experi-angelicalism'

Stories like this are not surprising when you consider the cultural waters in which we are swimming, ones that we have described throughout this book. As we explored in Chapters 5 and 7, just about the most significant cultural story of our time is expressive individualism. You might not know it by its name, but you will know its mantras:

'You do you.'
'Be your authentic self.'
'Be true to your self.'
'Live your truth.'

This pervasive idea runs through almost every social media feed, advertising campaign and Hollywood script. We breathe its fumes every day: meaning, purpose and truth are found within you and your primary goal should be to live these values out in the world. Expressive individualism then contributes to a deepening mistrust of authority from external sources as we don't want to let anyone tell us what to do where this conflicts with us living our own truth. Our friends Jo Frost and Peter Lynas write, 'We seek to be true to ourselves rather than forced to conform to society, previous generations or religion.'[1]

As followers of Jesus, we are compelled to construct our view of God, ourselves and the world from what he says, not primarily from our own feelings. If the call of the gospel is to be evangelical, the relentless beckoning of our world is to be 'experi-angelical.' This is hard for everyone. We all have cultural influences that shape how we view things. It is important that we ask the Lord to give us his eyes on what is the right thing and rather than our own

---

1 Frost and Lynas, *Being Human*, p. 8.

insights. When Jesus turns the tables in Luke 19, the disciples can't see as acutely what the problem is. Their cultural lenses have led to accepting societal norms. It is so much easier to see what is wrong in a culture that is not our own, because we do not inhabit that space. We need to pray that our cultural lenses might be removed so we can see with the eyes of Jesus.

As we articulated right at the beginning, in Chapter 1, experience is one of the sources we draw from when we develop our theology, alongside tradition, reason and Scripture. It is an important lens. God has given us senses through which we encounter him and interpret the world he has made. But as culture is increasingly obsessed with looking inward and outward, our primary authority must be upward. Jesus' parable of the two builders reminds us that if we want to live on a rock we must listen to his words and put them into practice (Matthew 7:24–27). And the perils of chiefly relying on ourselves are highlighted by the Old Testament prophet Jeremiah, 'The heart is deceitful above all things and beyond cure. Who can understand it?' (Jeremiah 17:9). Our human experience must always be read through the lens of Scripture.

In so many ways, we understand the temptation to adopt a theology with closer alignment to the winds of culture. It is understandable on a personal level. There is a natural inclination to shape our view of God around what we are like; we form our deity to look like us, think like us and agree with our value system. As Mark Twain quipped, 'God created man in his own image. And man, being a gentleman, returned the favour.'[2]

It is understandable on a relational level. The further the prevailing worldview departs from a biblical one, the more unpalatable the beliefs of Jesus-followers will become to some. None of us want to be rejected by our friends or family. Where we disagree with them on social issues, the temptation to compromise our theology is real.

---

2 Quoted in D. Dewr, *Sacred Paths for Modern Men: A wake up call from your 12 archetypes* (Woodbury: Llewellyn Publications, 2007).

The rise in cancel culture and the growing tendency to refuse to associate with anyone who challenges our value system heaps on the pressure in this area. Furthermore, for many the pressure to conform comes in the workplace, where many can feel holding, let alone expressing, a biblical worldview may cost them their job, or at the very least, favour and promotion.

And for many organisations and leaders, it is understandable on a pragmatic level. Having worked in the charity sector for several decades between us, we have seen good organisations adjust their statements of faith to remove exclusive faith claims that might cause offence – or drop their Christian distinctive entirely. This may make them more attractive to some sources of funding and favour, but significantly leads to long-term mission drift.

For all the above reasons, we sometimes wish we could change our convictions to reflect our culture. It would be a lot easier to be a part of the 'Experi-angelical' Alliance. We would be eligible for more government funding, have less awkward conversations and probably have more followers on social media if we could preach that everyone went to heaven, all roads lead to God, there were no limits in relationships so long as you didn't hurt anyone and the most important thing was to be true to yourself.

But while we understand the appeal of putting our experience on an equal footing of theological authority to the Bible, the Bible itself does not allow us to. And it is not a new problem. Paul in his letter to Timothy recognises our temptation to change Scripture to reflect how we feel:

> For the time will come when people will not put up with sound doctrine. Instead, to suit their own desires, they will gather around them a great number of teachers to say what their itching ears want to hear.
> (2 Timothy 4:3)

We understand how strong these feelings can be but we must do all we can to stand for truth in a world that wants to deconstruct it.

As we have sought to communicate in this book, we really believe that we are living in a time when it is absolutely fundamental that we hold our nerve theologically as the Church. There are so many temptations, trip wires and opportunities for compromise and we need to resist these with all we have. The Church is called to stand uncompromisingly on Scripture and to change our culture with the truth on the pages of the Bible – not baptise our culture and change the Bible to suit a secular landscape. We must stand firm!

For the sake of the world

At the same time, we must not just enjoy theological correctness while ignoring a world that does not know Jesus. The individualistic waters that we swim in can persuade us to believe that because we are righteous before God and right-thinking in belief, then what does it matter about those around us? But there is a world around us in need and the only hope is Jesus. As I, Gavin, try to articulate this, I encourage people to think about what their lives would be like if they did not know a Saviour, if they were still prodigals in a far-off land. Or if they were sheep without a shepherd:

> The LORD is not my shepherd, I am constantly without.
> I have no place of peace to lay my head.
> I can never find the tranquillity of still waters or refreshment
>   for my soul.
> I constantly choose the wrong path, I have no guide.
> When I face danger, or even death,
> I am overcome with paralysing fear for I am profoundly
>   alone.
> There is no one to protect or contend for me, comfort is
>   nowhere to be found.

There is no table for me to gather around,
I am overcome by my enemies who surround me wherever I
    look.
I am not anointed, my cup is bone dry.
All that follows me is grief and despair all the days of my life.
I will dwell away from the LORD forever.

When we are described as 'sheep' in Scripture, it hardly feels like a compliment. Sheep try to go their own way and are perhaps not the most intelligent of creatures. What they profoundly need is a shepherd to steer them on the right course and be there for them in all things. The truth, comfort and encouragement of Psalm 23 is so well known to us Christians. It is a testimony of a sheep with a shepherd. However, if you turn all of the positives of that passage into negatives you instead find the testimony of a sheep without a shepherd. This version is heartbreaking and is a further motivation to us both to help as many people as we can to find the Good Shepherd too.

The reality is that millions today wander without a shepherd. So many walk in darkness on shifting sand, not knowing that there is a firm place to stand amidst the uncertainty. Our neighbours and friends feel the weight of the permacrisis and live in a vacuum of hope.

The time is now

I, Phil, was speaking at a church in Sheffield that was planted around ten years ago and has experienced explosive growth among all generations, but particularly among students and young adults. It was a full-on day of ministry, the kind I am fond of, with a packed all-age service, lunch with a room full of spiritually (and physically) hungry young adults talking evangelism, and a recording of the church's podcast in the afternoon. By the time the evening service came around, I had been well fed, watered and caffeinated and was ready to go again.

That evening something took place that has happened twice in over twenty years of preaching. During the worship, I felt the Holy Spirit tell me to change my talk, minutes before I was handed the microphone. For clarity, this is definitely the exception rather than the rule. I believe God is speaking to me just as much in the preparation time as the preceding moments before a talk is given but I had a compelling sense the Holy Spirit was asking me to change tack and preach from Lamentations 3 rather than the Acts passage I had prepared. God's voice and presence felt so irresistible in that moment that I felt it would almost be disobedient not to listen to what he was saying and act. So, I nervously leaned across to the church leader and explained what I thought was happening. He replied, 'I was having a similar sense and there are a lot of non-Christians here tonight. I think we need to go in fairly early with a gospel response.' The last song finished. I left my notes on my chair, opened my Bible to the Old Testament passage and prayed, 'Lord, this has to be you. I don't have the words.'

I remember a couple of things that I communicated as a vessel that night. The first was a call to repent. Lamentations 3:40–42 speaks of acknowledging our sin and rebellion, examining our ways and returning to the Lord. The second was the offer of comfort for those trampled in the dust (3:16), with downcast souls (3:20) and in the depths of the pit (3:55). I suddenly then realised I was speaking less than a mile from the restaurant where I had received the news in a phone call in 2004 that my dad had died. I was not planning on telling that story, but it seemed the Spirit wanted it to be told.

After the talk, in response, two remarkable things happened. First, a young man asked me if I could pray with him. Through tears, he asked, 'Did you say you were twenty-one when your dad died?' I nodded. 'I'm twenty-two,' he said. 'My dad died last year.

Will you pray for me?' He was one of a heartbreaking number who wanted to acknowledge they were in the storm of life and wanted to know God's presence. Second, the pastor was right that, for whatever reason, there were a lot of non-Christians present. To the mid-talk gospel appeal, twelve young men and women gave their hearts to Jesus.

As I drove back down the M1, my heart both broken for the young man and bursting with joy celebrating souls saved, I was reminded again of the need to always be ready to go for it with the good news. Today is the day of salvation.

The current opportunities to share the gospel are profound. As we have explored, many are coming to faith in Jesus in ways old and new. Will we play our part in their stories? According to our latest *Talking Jesus* report (2022), one in three non-Christians wants to know more about Jesus after a conversation with a Christian friend about the hope they have.[3] How profoundly encouraging! What openness! For the new *Finding Jesus* 2025 report, we needed to find 100 people who had become Christians as adults in the last five years who were willing to be asked about their journey to faith. We were inundated with almost 300. We have prayed so long for a mighty move of God in the UK and right now we have the cultural openness to it. There is a chance for all Christians to be involved and an imperative that we are all released to reach our own personal one in three who is open to the gospel.

We are both naturally evangelistic but even we have noticed a tangible growth in interest and openness to the message of the gospel. As we have shared throughout these chapters, we are seeing many come to faith and are so encouraged.

At the same time, we are also encouraged by long-term fruit. Recently, I, Gavin, was speaking at an Assemblies of God (AOG) gathering. It was a joy to be among a large crowd of enthusiastic

3 *Talking Jesus* (2022), p. 26.

Pentecostals and at the end I had a wonderful conversation with a church leader. He reminded me that, twenty years earlier, I had spoken at a youth camp in a field in the east of England one warm August morning. This leader had been a teenager in that crowd and he had surrendered his life to Jesus at the end of the morning session. What a joy it was to hear this so many years on.

However, the story got better. I had spoken at the youth camp again in the evening and this time the challenge had been to respond to a call to ministry. This guy was ready to take that plunge too – after only a few hours of being a Christian. He responded to the call and spent the next twenty years living it out. During this time, he had been involved in youth ministry himself, had helped plant a few churches and was now leading a thriving church. I was utterly blown away by what the Lord can do in and through someone when he gets hold of a life. I found myself overcome with gratitude to Jesus as I listened to the guy explaining how, twenty years on, he was going for it more than ever, loved Jesus with all his heart and was leading a thriving church. How wonderful!

Hold tight. And go for it!

So, let's hold to biblical truth and rigour but also step up and acknowledge the simultaneous need to go for it with all we have in wholeheartedly sharing the gospel. There are great theologians who do not know a non-Christian and equally many people who want to share the gospel but do not know the Bible. In our day, we need both in tandem and to drive forward with them together.

We need to hold our nerve theologically and go for it with the gospel.

Some parts of the Church are pushing for increasingly progressive and liberal views, which often downplay the concept of sin, lean towards universalism and diminish the importance of a death-defeating, risen King. We feel that the role of evangelicals in transforming the spiritual health of the UK is to provide an uncompromising, evangelical, theological identity that springboards from this to share our hope with all around us.

This captivating mandate is at the heart of the postures we have described in this book. It also sums up our ten-year direction as the Evangelical Alliance. And it is encapsulated by David in the songbook of the Bible. He declares with joy that his salvation has given him a firm foundation:

> I waited patiently for the LORD;
>> he turned to me and heard my cry.
> He lifted me out of the slimy pit,
>> out of the mud and mire;
> he set my feet on a rock
>> and gave me a firm place to stand.
> (Psalm 40:1–2)

But then he recognises that the solid ground beneath his feet gives him a story to tell, a song to sing, a cause to live for, a fire in his heart and a mission to carry out:

> He put a new song in my mouth,
>> a hymn of praise to our God.
> Many will see and fear the LORD
>> and put their trust in him.
> (Psalm 40:3)

Our aim in these pages has been to encourage you of the beauty and benefit of the firm foundation on which we stand in Jesus. We hope you can stand a little taller upon the truth of Scripture, knowing you are surrounded and supported by a great cloud of witnesses, and part of a global family and an eternal story. And we are praying for you that you would be inspired to live and speak in a way that brings light into the darkness, life to the dying and hope to the hopeless.

We are good news people in a bad news world.

Our currency is hope. We bear it to a world in need. And hope has a name, and his name is Jesus.

Appendix: The Evangelical Alliance today

In every generation, the Evangelical Alliance has needed to adapt to its moment in order to be culturally impactful. The substance of who we are never changes. Since our formation in 1846, we have really only existed to fulfil the aims outlined in Chapter 3. But in this season, these core purposes take shape around four key areas: unity, gospel, voice and membership.

Unity

First, we are a unity organisation. We long to unite evangelicals around a shared basis of faith and desired purpose to see the United Kingdom won for Jesus. Unity is not uniformity. We want to celebrate the diversity of evangelicalism across ethnicities, age groups and beyond.

In their book, *Healing the Divides*, Jason Roach and Jessamin Birdsall say that they, 'believe that the Church is called to be a place where people of all cultures, languages, skin tones and histories can participate, grow and serve together.'[1] Though there is much work still to do, there are already beautiful examples of this.

- We gather leaders from across the different evangelical church streams in each of the four nations of the UK, seeing and hearing from hundreds of different leaders face to face each year.

---

1 J. Roach and J. Birdsall, *Healing the Divides: How every Christian can advance God's vision for racial unity and justice* (Epsom: The Good Book Company, 2022), p. 11.

- We have a One People Commission that seeks to foster unity across all ethnicities. This is an incredible work that is growing all the time and also incorporates our South Asian Forum. The diversity of UK evangelicalism is amazing but we still long for more that the world might be drawn towards this.
- Our UK Council and national executives are made up of representatives from all across the UK evangelical spectrum and they speak into our work and help us to unite and represent UK evangelicalism as widely as possible.

Gospel

Second, we are people of the 'evangel' – good news people driven by the gospel and its life-changing message. We want to see this shared with as many people as possible.

- We seek to serve evangelicals by giving them a roadmap as to what is going on nationally. We do this through work such as *Talking Jesus* or our recent *Finding Jesus* research. These help give great insight to leaders locally as to the landscape for the gospel at this time.
- We provide training and resources from within our membership, and for our membership, through our perspective gatherings and Great Commission resources hub.
- We train a new younger generation of public leaders in what it means to be good news for Jesus in every aspect of their lives from the secular workplace to their social time.
- We provide evangelistic speakers for local churches and events.

Voice

Third, voice matters to us. We want to provide a united voice into the media, into government and across all four parliaments of the

United Kingdom. We want to keep speaking up and speaking out in a hopeful and realistic way and in a manner that challenges some of the accepted social narratives of our day that are in conflict with the message of Jesus.

- Our advocacy team have hundreds of meetings a year with MPs and organisations across the four nations of the UK in order to provide a united evangelical voice into the corridors of power.
- Our team carries the voices of the UK Church into the media, speaking in these settings regularly.
- We help local churches and individual Christians to speak up themselves and train many people to do this each year.
- We remind Christians of their religious freedom and of the opportunities to speak up and out into society.

Membership

Fourth, we have always been a membership organisation, made up of churches, organisations and individuals. There were 3,000 founder members, which had grown to 6,000 people by 1859. After the rapid growth in the 1990s, individual numbers dipped to around 13,000. Since reemphasising personal membership in the last few years, we have seen comparable rapid growth to the late twentieth century and numbers are back in excess of 27,000. At the current rate, we hope to double in size over the next decade. This growth would dramatically increase the volume of our voice in the media and the corridors of power on issues that matter to evangelical Christians.

We long to see our membership grow and connect and represent our members. We can only speak up for those who are with us and we can only drive forward with those who are part of us.

Both of us started out serving for over a decade at Youth for Christ. One of the mindset shifts we had to adopt when we joined the Evangelical Alliance was moving from a purely mission agency to a membership organisation. We exist primarily for the benefit of our members, so will seek to promote their activities rather than beginning things that compete or duplicate what others are doing. We were both used to putting things on the table to help the Church reach young people. We have had to get used to a posture in which we primarily seek to provide the table itself, supporting, unifying and linking likeminded churches, organisations and individuals.

- We are currently welcoming in thousands of new members per year. We have over 3,000 church members, 500 organisational members and 27,000 individual members.
- We serve, support and tell the stories of our membership widely.
- We provide resources that are needed and wanted by our membership to serve their needs and requirements as they seek to be the good news people needed in our cultural moment.

We want to move forward as the Evangelical Alliance needed in our day, focusing on the main thing, not deviating from our calling, and serving the Church as we together make Jesus known.

Evangelical Alliance

The Evangelical Alliance is made up of hundreds of organisations, thousands of churches and tens of thousands of individuals, joined together for the sake of the gospel. Representing our members since 1846, the Evangelical Alliance is the oldest and largest evangelical unity movement in the UK.

United in mission and voice, we exist to serve and strengthen the work of the church in our communities and throughout society. Highlighting the significant opportunities and challenges facing the church today, we work together to resource Christians so that they are able to act upon their faith in Jesus, to speak up for the gospel, justice and freedom in their areas of influence.

Working across the UK, with offices in London, Cardiff, Stockport, Glasgow and Belfast, our members come together from across denominations, locations, age groups and ethnicities, all sharing a passion to know Jesus and make Him known.

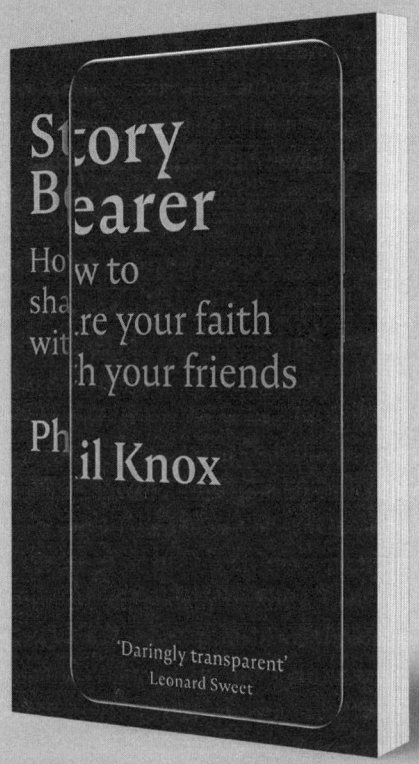